THE PENGUIN

FOUNDER EDITOR (19

Editor: Betty

EINHARD was born of noble parents in the Main valley, towards A.D. 770. He was educated in the monastery of Fulda, and soon after 791 was sent by Abbot Baugolf to the Palace School of Charlemagne at Aachen. He became the adviser and personal friend of Charlemagne, and remained so until the Emperor's death in 814. He was also in high favour with Lewis the Pious, Charlemagne's son and successor. In 830 he retired to Seligenstadt, and he died in 840. In addition to *The Life of Charlemagne*, written between 829 and 836, there survive three works by Einhard: the *Letters*, *On the Translation and the Miracles of SS. Marcellinus and Petrus*, and *On the Adoration of the Cross*.

NOTKER THE STAMMERER and THE MONK OF SAINT GALL are probably the same person, although this cannot be proved. The author of *Charlemagne*, this second book about the Emperor and his family, was born in the Thur valley, near Lake Constance, towards A.D. 840. He wrote his book of anecdotes for the Emperor Charles the Fat, Charlemagne's epileptic great-grandson, between 884 and 887. His whole adult life seems to have been passed in the Benedictine monastery of Saint Gall. Notker died in 912, and this fits the few facts known about the Monk.

LEWIS THORPE, B.A., L.-ès-L., Ph.D., D. de l'U., LL.D., F.I.A.L., F.R.S.A., F.R.Hist.S., was Professor of French at Nottingham University from 1958 to 1977. He joined the staff of that university in 1946 after distinguished war service. He was President of the British Branch of the International Arthurian Society, and editor of the Society's *Bulletin Bibliographique*. He was also editor of *Nottingham Mediaeval Studies* and *Nottingham French Studies*. He published many articles, and his books include *La France guerrière* (1945), *Le Roman de Laurin, fils de Marques le Sénéchal* (1950), *Le Roman de Laurin, text of MS B.N.f.fr. 22548* (1960), *Guido Farina, Painter of Verona, 1896–1957* (1967), with Barbara Reynolds, *Einhard the Frank: The Life of Charlemagne* (1970), *Le Roman de Silence*, by Heldris de Cornuälle (1972) and *The Bayeux Tapestry and the Norman Invasion* (1973). He also translated *Geoffrey of Monmouth: The History of the Kings of Britain*, *Gregory of Tours: The History of the Franks* and *Gerald of Wales: The Journey through Wales and The Description of Wales* for the Penguin Classics. Lewis Thorpe was a member of the M.C.C. He died on 10 October 1977.

EINHARD
AND
NOTKER THE STAMMERER

Two Lives of Charlemagne

TRANSLATED
WITH AN INTRODUCTION BY
LEWIS THORPE

*

PENGUIN BOOKS

Penguin Books Ltd, Harmondsworth, Middlesex, England
Penguin Books, 625 Madison Avenue, New York, New York 10022, U.S.A.
Penguin Books Australia Ltd, Ringwood, Victoria, Australia
Penguin Books Canada Ltd, 2801 John Street, Markham, Ontario, Canada L3R 1B4
Penguin Books (N.Z.) Ltd, 182–190 Wairau Road, Auckland 10, New Zealand

—

This translation first published 1969
Reprinted 1971, 1972, 1974, 1976, 1977, 1979

—

Made and printed in Great Britain
by Richard Clay (The Chaucer Press) Ltd,
Bungay, Suffolk
Set in Monotype Bembo

FOR ADRIAN THORPE

CONTENTS

Einhard

THE LIFE OF CHARLEMAGNE

CONTENTS

Notker the Stammerer, Monk of Saint Gall

CHARLEMAGNE

INTRODUCTION

I. CHARLEMAGNE, KING AND EMPEROR

The sources of our knowledge

Charles the Great, King of the Franks and later ruler of the Carolingian Empire, may at first sight seem comparable with that other famous medieval figure, Arthur of Britain, for in both cases the fictional hero into which each later developed tends to obscure the original historical personage. Of the real Arthur we know very little, although most historians and students of literature accept that he was a Romano-British guerrilla leader who lived in the district called Strathclyde in the first half of the sixth century. The fact that the literary Charlemagne is the central figure of a vast series of epic poems written in France in the eleventh, twelfth and thirteenth centuries, and of a corpus of derived literature in Germany, Italy and elsewhere, must not encourage us to think that of him, too, considered as a real person, we know as little as we do of the historical Arthur. In effect, our knowledge of Charles the Great is both extensive and detailed.

In the present book it is of the historical Charles that we shall be thinking and not of the legendary Charlemagne. It is, however, customary to speak of the historical king and emperor as Charlemagne, and to this habit we must defer. Charlemagne is the form to which the oblique case of his Latin name, *Carolus Magnus*, was reduced two hundred years and more after his death, in the French *chansons-de-geste*. Could he hear us using it, Charles would no doubt laugh his quiet laugh, measure a few thousand of the Aquitani with his sword[1] and send the ringleaders to spend the remainder of their lives in remote monasteries: for he was a Frank and, if he spoke Latin and understood a little Greek, his own language was Frankish and his blood Teutonic.

Our knowledge of the life and reign of Charlemagne is obtained from a long series of contemporary documents, only the most important of which can be mentioned here. We possess in particular three series of chronicles, called the *Annales regni Francorum*, covering the period 741–829; a revision of these *Annales regni Francorum*, for 741–801; and the *Annales Mosellani*, or Moselle Annals, for 703–797. There is also a number of other annals of lesser importance, those of Murbach, Lorsch, Saint-Amand, Fulda, Salzburg, etc. Secondly, we have the corpus of some eighty capitularies of Charlemagne, the *Capitularia regni Francorum*. There is, thirdly, the correspondence of the Carolingian kings and emperors: the *Codex Carolinus*, containing the letters which they exchanged with the popes, and the more general *Epistolae Aevi Carolini*. We possess a long series of Latin lives of such contemporary figures as Adalhard, Alcuin, Liudger, Sturm, Wigbert and Willehad, with the two biographies of Charlemagne's successor, Lewis the Pious, by Thegan, Bishop of Trier, and the so-called Limousin Astronomer. To these must be added such works as the *Liber de Episcopis Mettensibus*, or *History of the Bishops of Metz*, by Paul the Deacon, and the anonymous *Gesta Abbatum Fontanellensium*, or annals of the abbots of Fontenelle. Lastly we have two biographies, or pseudo-biographies, of Charlemagne himself: the *Vita Caroli* by Einhard, written between 829 and 836; and the much more discursive and anecdotal *De Carolo Magno*, written for Charles the Fat, in 883–4, some seventy years after Charlemagne's death, by the Monk of Saint Gall. These last two documents form the subject of this book.

The military campaigns

Charlemagne was born *c.* 742 as the eldest son of Pepin the Short and his wife Bertrada. He had a younger brother, Carloman, who was born *c.* 751, and there had been a third brother, Pepin, who had died as a child. There was also a sister, Gisela, born in 757. Until 754 Pepin the Short was Mayor of the Palace under Childeric III, the last of the Merovingian kings. In the winter of 753–4 and the following spring, Pope Stephen II travelled slowly from Rome to Saint Denis, outside Paris, and there, on 28 July 754, with his own hands, crowned Pepin the Short as King of the Franks and appointed his two sons Charlemagne and Carloman as his joint heirs. By this single act the Pope at once deposed Childeric III and put an end to the Merovingian dynasty, brought into being as its replacement the dynasty of the Carolingian kings and emperors, and sought for himself an ally against the emperors in Constantinople and the Longobards in northern Italy. After his coronation King Pepin the Short lived for a further fourteen years. Immediately before his death at Saint Denis on 24 September 768, he divided his lands between his two sons.

To understand the military aims and achievements of Charlemagne, it is necessary to have a clear conception of the extent of these territories.[2] They stretched from the River Saal on the eastern borders of Thuringia and the River Danube on the southern frontier of the Bavarian Nordgau almost to the northern shores of modern Holland; from the River Lech and the Graian Alps in the south-east to the entire Atlantic seaboard of modern France, excluding Brittany; from the Frisian Islands in the north to the Pyrenees and the Mediterranean in the south. In terms of modern countries they included much of Germany, most of Holland, the whole of Belgium and Switzerland, and almost the whole of France. In contemporary terms, from east to west, they included the Bavarian Nordgau, Thuringia, Hesse, Alamania (= Swabia), Austrasia, Frisia,

Burgundia, Provincia, Septimania, Neustria and Aquitania. To the north they were bordered by the lands of the Saxons, to the east by Bavaria, to the south-east by the kingdom of the Longobards, which ran from the Alps to the southern frontier of Tuscany, and to the south, over the Pyrenees, by the Emirate of Cordova.

The centre and south of this vast area was given to Carloman: Alamania, Burgundia, Provincia, Septimania and eastern Aquitania. To Charlemagne was apportioned a great half-circle running westwards from Ratisbon on the Danube and from the River Saal, through the Bavarian Nordgau, Thuringia, Hesse, Austrasia and Frisia to the North Sea, and then southwards through Neustria and western Aquitania to the Pyrenees.

The disparity of personality and experience between the two brothers at the moment of their succession was very great. Charlemagne was about twenty-six and, although he had never held great authority, he had been associated with his father in most of the events of the last few years of his life. Carloman was a boy of about seventeen. Both born of the same parents, Charlemagne is supposed to have been a love-child, while Carloman was legitimate. As we see him through the accounts of later writers who were for the most part his dependants, Charlemagne was a man of limitless energy, great resolution and considerable personal strength; Carloman, seen through the prejudiced eyes of these same writers, appears to have been peevish, given to self-pity and the easy victim of the flatterers who surrounded him.

The period immediately following 768 was largely occupied by problems which the two young kings, and Charlemagne in particular, had inherited from their father, but to these Charlemagne added a domestic complication of his own and his mother's making. During the last years of the reign of King Pepin, Aquitaine had been in revolt. In 769 a certain Hunold led a new rising of the Aquitanians of the south-west in Saintonge and Poitou. Charlemagne moved with his army towards the southern reaches of his inheritance, met his brother Carloman at Moncontour and was refused assistance by him. The revolt of the Aquitanians was put down, but Charlemagne never saw his brother again. With the help of their mother Bertrada, relations were patched up between them, for an open quarrel would have been of no advantage to either of the Frankish kings. Then, to what must have been the considerable relief of Charlemagne, Carloman died suddenly in December 771. His vassals immediately did homage to Charlemagne and the entire territory of Pepin the Short was thus united once more under one ruler. Charlemagne then turned to face new difficulties in the east. In 770, at the persuasion of his mother and to the great annoyance of Pope Stephen III, he had married the daughter of Desiderius, King of the Longobards; a year later he dismissed his young wife and in her place married the Swabian Hildigard; on the death of Carloman in 771, that King's widow Gerberga and her young sons joined Charlemagne's repudiated wife at the court of this same Desiderius in Pavia; after a brief period of alliance with Rome, Desiderius quarrelled with Pope Stephen III; and to aggravate all these circumstances, which were difficult enough for Charlemagne in all conscience, Desiderius saw a deadly threat to his own Longobard kingdom in the junction of the dead Carloman's territories with those of his formidable brother. Charlemagne assembled his forces at Geneva, crossed the Alps and in October 773 began to besiege Pavia, the capital of Desiderius and his Longobard kingdom. The city fell in June 774, Desiderius was deposed and Charlemagne added a new territory to those which he already possessed. During the siege of Pavia, he moved on to Rome, met Pope Hadrian I, the successor to Stephen III, and renewed the Donation of Pepin by which the Frankish kings confirmed to the popes the possession of all territories nominally under their sway.

With the revolt in Aquitaine crushed, Carloman dead and
his lands engulfed, Desiderius beaten and his Longobard kingdom captured, and with relations established on a firm footing
with the Papacy, Charlemagne had already turned to face a
long series of most bloodthirsty wars with the Saxons in the
north. These were to continue intermittently from 772 until
804, for a period of more than thirty years. The major campaigns were those of 772, 775, 776, 779, 782, 783, 784–5, 794,
796, 797–8 and 804. It is impossible for us to follow all these
wars in detail. In 772 Charlemagne crossed the River Eder and
the River Diemel and destroyed the Irminsul, the sacred pillar
of wood, 'the all-sustaining pillar' of the Saxons. In 775 he
crossed the River Weser and attacked the Ostphalians. After
the campaign of 776 he occupied much of Westphalia. In 779
he beat Witikind at Bochult, called a general assembly at
Lippspringe and divided part of Saxonia into mission districts.
In 782 the Saxons rebelled against this Cartulary of Charlemagne and nearly five thousand were massacred at Verden.
From then on year after year saw new revolts and rebellions,
new massacres, temporary submissions, vast deportations. In
794 Charlemagne deported seven thousand Saxons, in 797
every third household, in 798 sixteen hundred leaders. In 797
he issued the second Saxon Cartulary. Only in 804 was
Saxonia finally conquered and pacified.

During this long period of the Saxon wars, Charlemagne
had many military preoccupations elsewhere. In 775–6 Rotgaud, the Longobard Duke of Friuli, aggravated beyond endurance by the territorial claims of Charlemagne's ally, Pope
Hadrian I, revolted but was killed in battle. In 778 Charlemagne crossed the Pyrenees into Spain, penetrated as far south
as Saragossa, which he failed to take, destroyed the walls of
Pamplona and, as he moved back into Aquitania, suffered the
defeat to his rearguard known as the battle of Roncevaux.
Duke Tassilo III of Bavaria, who had been in revolt against
Pepin the Short years before and whose wife Liutberga was

one of the daughters of Desiderius, the deposed King of the Longobards, conspired with his brother-in-law, Areghis, but was finally forced to surrender and, like Desiderius before him, sent to a monastery in 788. As Charlemagne and his armies forced their way ever deeper into the lands of the Saxons, they gradually began to join battle with peoples who lived even farther to the east, the Abotrites, the Wiltzes, the Sorbs, the Avars, the Wends and, more to the south, the Slavs. In the west the Carolingian leader Audulf won a victory against the Bretons in 786, as did Wido in 799, and a year later the Breton leaders met at Tours and offered their allegiance to Charlemagne; but by 811 they were in revolt once more. In the north Godefrid, King of the Northmen, who had watched the successive reduction of the Saxons and the Abotrites, and then the fighting with the Wiltzes, built an immense earthen rampart called the Danework south of the River Eider, from the Baltic to the North Sea. In 808 he mounted a campaign against the Franks, and in 810 he sent a huge fleet to ravage the Frisian Islands. Charlemagne, who was then nearly seventy, marched northwards to meet Godefrid at Verden, but before the two forces could join battle the Danish leader was murdered. It was Charlemagne's last expedition.

Diplomacy and administration

From the joint accession in 768 until this final campaign against Godefrid the Northman in 810, the reign of Charlemagne was one long and never-ending series of warlike enterprises. In the midst of all this military activity, and largely because of it, he was at the same time engaged in diplomatic relations with the rulers of many other lands. Irene, joint ruler of the Empire in Constantinople, in 781 proposed a marriage between her infant son, the Emperor Constantine VI, and Charlemagne's daughter Rotrude, but this was eventually broken off six years later. From 789 to 796 Charlemagne was in correspondence with Offa, King of Mercia; and Eardulf, King of Northum-

bria, visited him as a fugitive in Nimeguen in 808. His relations with Harun-al-Rachid are mentioned in some detail by
Einhard and the Monk of Saint Gall: he sent envoys to
Bagdad in 797 and 807, and messengers from Harun arrived
at Ivrea in 801 and Aachen in 807. In 803 the Emperor
Nicephorus I, who had succeeded the Empress Irene in the
previous year, sent an embassy to Charlemagne. In the course
of the single year 810 Charlemagne concluded peace treaties
with Nicephorus I, with El Hakem the Cruel, Emir of
Cordova, and with Hemming, King of the Danes, who had
succeeded to his father Godefrid.

Four times Charlemagne visited Rome: in 774, during the
siege of Pavia, when he was welcomed by Pope Hadrian I; in
781, when Hadrian crowned the two young princes, Pepin and
Lewis, as Kings of the Longobards and the Aquitanians; in
787, when Charlemagne spent Easter with the Pope; and in
800 when, on Christmas Day, Pope Leo III crowned Charlemagne as Emperor.

All this activity, both military and civil, spread over territory so extensive in days when travelling was so difficult,
demanded a complicated administrative machine at the centre,
if it was to be successful. In the years following his coronation
Charlemagne devoted his attention largely to administrative
problems. Each year saw new additions to the code of laws
contained in the corpus of capitularies. Most of the reforms
concerned the administration of justice; but at the same time
the military system was changed radically. Charlemagne could
not afford a standing army: but now the obligation of periodic
military service was moved from the individual to the land
held. The production of a suitably armed soldier for a specified
period was henceforth the responsibility of the holder or
holders, few or numerous, of a given piece of land, who chose,
paid and equipped their nominee. New edicts were announced
to provincial assemblies by Charlemagne's *missi dominici*, or
royal commissioners, pairs of unpaid emissaries, of high rank,

one a churchman, one a layman, sent out on circuit to a given neighbourhood. Failure to observe the edicts was tried by local law-courts, consisting of seven *scabini* or jurymen, elected for life; and the equity of the decisions of the *scabini* was supervised by the local count. In 802 Charlemagne reduced to writing the various national codes. All of this must have seemed much better to the court official writing it down on parchment in Aachen than it did to the individual of some far-flung township in the Carolingian Empire. The laws were often inequitable and unjust; the *scabini* did not understand the laws and were, in any case, afraid of the local count; the *missi* were busy men, who had heavy commitments and responsibilities at home and could ill afford these long excursions on circuit; the provincial assemblies listened to the new edicts, signified their assent without too much effort of comprehension, and then, on the departure of the *missi*, continued to act exactly as they had always acted before; so many men of talent were needed at the centre to set out and promulgate the laws that there were too few men of talent left on the periphery to see that they were observed; and those who planned the laws were often out of touch with reality. These are problems common to all centralized governments.

The Carolingian Renaissance

Charlemagne himself was illiterate: Einhard describes his rather pathetic attempts to learn to write, but concludes that, 'although he tried very hard, he had begun too late in life and he made little progress'.[3] His own language was Frankish; as we have seen, he spoke Latin well and understood some Greek.[4] He learned the elements of grammar from Peter the Deacon, and Alcuin taught him rhetoric, dialectic, mathematics and astrology. His respect for learning and the liberal arts seems to have been genuine and deep-rooted. The Monk of Saint Gall describes at length Charlemagne's interest in church liturgy and music, and his careful insistence on the proper chanting of the responses and the reading of the lessons, but he may well be transferring to the Emperor some of his own personal enthusiasms. Gradually, as the years passed, Charlemagne assembled at his court in Aachen many of the most learned men of Europe. In 781 he met again in Parma the Englishman Alcuin, who had previously visited his court. From 782 to 796 Alcuin was at Aachen, and from then until his death in 804 he lived in his abbey of Saint Martin in Tours. Some time before the conquest of the Longobard kingdom in 785, Charlemagne had come into contact with Paul the Deacon, Peter of Pisa and Paulinus, later of Aquileia. Einhard, a Frank born in the Maingau, moved to the Palace School in Aachen in 791. These men, and others like them, were the mainsprings of the Carolingian Renaissance. During his years at Aachen, Alcuin organized the Palace School. Under Alcuin the school became an important factor in national life; it developed into a well defined and highly favoured institution. Any magnate might send his sons, nor were humble antecedents allowed to exclude a boy of talent. Plebeian or patrician, it mattered nothing to Charles: he singled out the most proficient with rare impartiality and promoted them to vacant offices or preferments. Alcuin taught in person and enlisted all the other literati in the service. The King set the fashion of taking lessons, and all his family were put to school. Being a court affair, the school accompanied the royal household in its wanderings. It was not hampered by elaborate paraphernalia. Alcuin sent envoys far and wide to purchase books for his pupils, but the library which he gathered must have been both small and portable. The primers of the elementary subjects – orthography, grammar, rhetoric and dialectic – were written by himself. They are extant and printed in his works.[5] Theology was seen as the centre of all learning. Students who had shown marked ability were sent out to become the abbots of Frankish monasteries. Great monastic schools were developed at Fulda and Tours, and later at Corbie, Saint Wandrille, Saint Gall and elsewhere. Latin was restored as a literary language, spelling was revised and penmanship remodelled on the old uncial letters. As H. W. Garrod wrote: 'The debt of literature to the Carolingian copying-schools may be best brought home to us by a very simple consideration. If we set aside Catullus, Tibullus, Propertius and Silius Italicus, together with the tragedies of Seneca and parts of Statius and Claudian, we owe the preservation of practically the whole of Latin poetry to the schools at the time of Charlemagne. These same scholars have preserved to us, except for Varro, Tacitus and Apuleius, practically the whole of the prose literature of Rome.'[6] Einhard tells us that Charlemagne also ordered the old sagas of the Frankish peoples to be written out, and that he began a grammar of his native tongue.[7]

The two lives by Einhard and the Monk of Saint Gall both contain references to the thermal baths at Aachen, the cathedral modelled on San Vitale in Ravenna, the Imperial palace and the great bridge constructed over the River Rhine at Mainz. These show yet another side of Charlemagne's immense creative activity.

*

Opinions vary still today as to the precise importance to us all of the long reign of Charlemagne. Would the history of the Christian church in Europe in the later Middle Ages and throughout the world in more recent times have been radically different had Charlemagne not fought his long series of wars against the Saxons and other peoples? Had Alcuin and his fellow scholars not achieved all that they did at Aachen and in the monasteries fostered and founded by Charlemagne, should we be without the rich literatures of medieval France and Germany? Without the Carolingian Renaissance would that other and much greater Renaissance, which lasted from Petrarch to Rabelais, Thomas More and Erasmus, have been possible? In a recent book Professor Donald Bullough has assembled an admirable collection of photographs of the buildings, manuscripts, reliquaries and other artistic productions of the Carolingian era.[8] Without these would the history of European architecture and fine art be completely different? Is the Empire which Charlemagne built up with such effort and which fell to pieces so soon after his death to be seen as an earlier form of the Empire of Napoleon Bonaparte, or of the group of Common Market countries in Europe in our own century? The answer probably is that all these things would have existed without Charlemagne, but that they would not be as we know them today. Certainly the achievements and personality of Charlemagne loom very large in the thinking of most modern Europeans. As a symbol of this thinking the *Prix Charlemagne* is awarded periodically to the woman or man who is considered to have done most to further the cause of a united Europe. As a further tribute, from 26 June until 19 September 1965, the Tenth Exhibition of the Council of Europe, organized in the Rathaus, Cathedral and Museum of the town of Aachen by Professor Wolfgang Braunfels, had as its subject Charlemagne; and some seven hundred objects connected with the great Emperor were lent to that Exhibition from public and private collections in Europe, the U.S.S.R. and the U.S.A.

2. EINHARD THE FRANK

We possess a considerable amount of information about Einhard, the author of the *Vita Caroli* or the *Life of Charlemagne*. In his introduction he tells us that Charlemagne was his master and patron, and that he had seen with his own eyes the happenings which he describes. His two immediate reasons for writing were the personal knowledge which he possessed of Charlemagne, and the debt of gratitude which he owed to this remarkable king and emperor, who had helped him to continue his education and with whom he had long lived on friendly terms. Apart from the plan which he proposes for his work, the text itself has no really personal touches. Of Charlemagne's birth and childhood he claims to have no knowledge (§4). He will shape his biography in this way: 'First of all I shall describe his achievements at home and abroad, then his personal habits and enthusiasms, then the way in which he administered his kingdom and last of all his death, omitting from all this nothing which ought to be known or, indeed, which is worthy of being recorded' (§4).

In his reticence, Einhard does not even name himself. This is remedied by a prologue written for *The Life of Charlemagne* by Walahfrid Strabo, Abbot of Reichenau,[9] and by information provided by other ninth-century writers who knew Einhard personally. He was a man of comparatively noble birth.[10] He was born in the Maingau.[11] His parents were called Einhart[12] and Engilfrit,[13] and during the abbacy of Baugolf (779–802) he was sent to be educated in the monastery of Fulda, in Hesse, some sixty miles north-east of Frankfurt, of which institution his father and mother were benefactors. A number of manuscripts written by Einhard while he was at Fulda still exist in the monastery and two of them are dated 19 April 788 and 12 September 791. Soon after 791 he was sent by Abbot Baugolf to the Palace School of Charlemagne at Aachen.[14] By his intelligence, wisdom and probity,[15] virtues which are rarely found united in the same man at any period in history, he soon made his mark at court, and became the adviser and personal friend of Charlemagne. Of the freedom with which Charlemagne came to discuss his affairs with Einhard, Walahfrid Strabo tells us in his prologue; and in his own introduction Einhard writes of 'the friendly relations which I enjoyed with him and his children from the moment when I first began to live at his court'. He seems to have been a man of many talents. In one of his letters to Charlemagne, Alcuin calls Einhard by the nickname Bezaleel, which the Emperor apparently used for him.[16] This nickname is repeated by

Walahfrid Strabo in a poem written in 829, long after the death of Charlemagne.[17] Alcuin himself had been given the name Flaccus and the two scholars and their friends addressed Charlemagne as David. If the name Bezaleel is to be taken at all seriously, it may imply that Einhard was skilled in metal work, wood-carving and the cutting of gems. From documents at Fontanelle and Fulda it has been argued that Angisus, who became Abbot of Saint-Germer-de-Flay in 807, had previously been in charge of public works at Aachen under the direction of Einhard;[18] and that Ratger, the third Abbot of Fulda (802–817), sent one of his monks called Brun to Aachen to be instructed by Einhard in the arts.[19]

Einhard seems to have been a very small man. Walahfrid Strabo calls him an '*homuncio*' in his prologue, and in his poem of 829 he uses the word '*homullus*'. In one of his poems Alcuin refers to Einhard as '*Nardulus*' and '*parvulus*':[20] he reminds his readers that, despite its lack of size, the bee makes fine honey; and that, for all its smallness, the pupil of the eye rules all our bodily functions.[21] As early as 796, Theodulf, Bishop of Orleans, had compared Einhard to a busy ant.[22]

After the death of Charlemagne in 814, Einhard remained in high favour with his successor, Lewis the Pious, a fact which clearly astonished Walahfrid Strabo.[23] It was at this period that he seems to have married Imma, the sister of Bernhard, Bishop of Worms and Abbot of Weissenburg.[24] His married state did not prevent Lewis from making him abbot of a long series of monasteries, Saint Pierre and Saint Bavon in Ghent, for example, Saint Servais in Maestricht and Saint Wandrille at Fontanelle. In 815 he was given a grant of lands at Michlinstat and at Mulinheim, later to be known as Seligenstadt, 'the city of the Saints', from the church which Einhard built there and the relics of Saint Marcellinus and Saint Peter which he had carried there. Gradually as the years passed his health began to fail. In letters dated 829 and 830 he wrote of pains in his stomach and his back, and in this latter year he left Aachen and went to live in Seligenstadt. Imma died in 836. The death of Einhard himself occurred on 14 March 840.

3. THE *VITA CAROLI* OF EINHARD

There are in existence four works written by Einhard, all of them in Latin: the *Vita Caroli*, of which a new translation is printed in this book; a series of seventy-one letters, called the *Einharti Epistolae*, which, as far as they can be dated, run from 814 to 840; the *De translatione et miraculis sanctorum suorum Marcellini et Petri*; and a book dedicated to Servatus Lupus, the *Libellus de adoranda Cruce*.

It is thought that *The Life of Charlemagne* was written between 829 and 836,[25] for it is first mentioned by this same Servatus Lupus, later Abbot of Ferrières (840–62), in a letter which he wrote at some unspecified moment between these two dates. This means, in all probability, that Einhard composed it after he had left Aachen and when he was living in comparative peace in Seligenstadt.

As we have seen, in his introduction Einhard states his aims: they are to write the public history of Charlemagne and to describe the Emperor's life and his day-to-day habits, omitting nothing which is relevant and yet remaining as succinct as possible. Walahfrid Strabo writes of 'the scrupulousness of the truth which he offered to the enquiring reader'; and Einhard himself says: 'I am very conscious of the fact that no one can describe these events more accurately than I, for I was present when they took place and, as they say, I saw them with my own eyes. What is more, I cannot be absolutely sure that these happenings will in fact ever be described by anyone else.' *The Life of Charlemagne* is, then, something with which we are most familiar in our own day: the memoirs of a former public servant who is now in retirement. It has already been made clear that in one way Einhard differs fundamentally from the writers of modern memoirs, for, far from explaining at inordinate length his own personal contribution to affairs of state during the period of contemporary history which he is describing, he does not even mention his own name. He was at Aachen from some time after 791 until the Emperor's death in 814; and he stayed on in high position at the Imperial Court, under Lewis the Pious, from 814 until 830. This gives a span of some forty years, during which he could have been closely connected with all public events and with all domestic happenings in the lives of the two Emperors. In 791 Charlemagne was forty-nine: §§13–17 of Book II, nearly everything in Book III, and the whole of the description of the Emperor's last years and death, together with the last will and testament, are therefore based upon such personal information as Einhard acquired during the twenty-three years which he spent in the service of Charlemagne. As Louis Halphen points out,[26] this was not the Charlemagne of the heroic period, the war in Italy, the war in Spain and the more exacting episodes of the wars against the Saxons. On the other hand, Einhard may well have had access to official documents which concerned events of the period 749–91, from the deposition of Childeric III until his own coming to court, and he would have been free to talk with older men who had lived through these events. That he used source-books is clear enough. Perhaps a third of what he has to say about the wars and foreign policy of Charlemagne is taken from the *Annales regni Francorum*, which were drawn up in their final form during the reign of Lewis the Pious.[27] At least five of his statements resemble closely comparable passages in the *Liber de Episcopis Mettensibus* by Paul the Deacon.[28] It is thought that the details which he gives in §§1–2 concerning the fall of the Merovingians and the rise of Pepin the Short may come from a lost source-book. As secretary to Lewis the Pious, he would be able to draw from the Imperial archives the details given in Bk. II, §§16 and 18, about Charlemagne's diplomatic relations with foreign potentates. If one accepts that he composed *The Life of Charlemagne* at Seligenstadt between the years 829 and 836, he wrote much of it from memory. He may have been using notes which he had compiled previously; some of his sources he may have had with him; of the last will and testament given in §33 he may have possessed a transcript.

Four things immediately strike one about *The Life of Charlemagne*, more particularly in view of what has been written in the previous paragraph: it is occasionally inaccurate in its data, and, in a number of ways, it seems deliberately to obscure the truth, always in favour of Charlemagne; the author never addresses us in person, except in the introduction; in view of the remarkable series of events which Einhard has to recount for us, his biography is extremely short; and, when viewed as a work of art, especially by those accustomed to considering the great masterpieces of European literature, in their correct sequence, over the last two thousand years, there is a strange perfection about it which becomes all the more unexpected when we remember that it was written in Seligenstadt in the 830s.

Inaccuracies of a purely factual nature will be referred to in the notes. On at least three occasions Einhard seems to feel a need to leave the reader without information which he was clearly in a position to give. In Bk. I, §§2–3, and Bk. III, §18, he is unwilling to analyse the political relations between Charlemagne and his brother Carloman; in a similar way, in Bk. II, §§6 and 11, and Bk. III, §18, we are left very much in the dark as to Charlemagne's treatment of his first wife and her father, Desiderius the Longobard; and in Bk. II, §11, Einhard is vague in the account of the Bavarian war of 787 and Charlemagne's relationship with Duke Tassilo. Whatever the rights and wrongs of these cases may have been, one suspects that on Charlemagne's side there was at least as much wrong as right, and that Einhard would have done little good to his hero's cause if he had revealed what he must have known about the fate of Carloman's wife Gerberga and her two sons, of Charlemagne's first wife and her father Desiderius and of Duke Tassilo. It has been suggested that Einhard's refusal in Bk. II, §4, to write about Charlemagne's early years may have been caused in part by the obvious embarrassment of the fact that the Emperor was seventy or seventy-two at his death in 814 and that his parents Pepin the Short and Bertrada were not married until 750. It is odd that, in Bk. III, §20, Einhard will not give the name of Charlemagne's mistress, the mother of Pepin the Hunchback, for in the *Liber de Episcopis Mettensibus* by Paul the Deacon, from which, as we have seen, he takes some of his material, she is clearly named as Himiltrude. He is similarly reticent in Bk. III, §19, about the indiscretions of Charlemagne's daughters.[29] The truth is, as he tells us in his introduction, that Einhard is writing a panegyric or what the Romans would have called an encomium of Charlemagne, and this in the lifetime of Charlemagne's son, Lewis the Pious, who had given to him the very lands in Seligenstadt in which he was living as he wrote. We must be warned that his information is not always reliable and that he will occasionally omit matters which it suits him to suppress, but we should not be surprised to find this in 'a book which perpetuates the memory of the greatest and most distinguished of men'.

In the twenty-three years which Einhard spent at Charlemagne's court he was on friendly terms with the Emperor. He seems, however, to have received very little material reward for his services, and it may well be that his role has been exaggerated. It was not until 815, the year after Charlemagne's death, that began the long list of abbeys and personal properties which were made over to him.[30] Twice at least he had played an apparently important part in the carrying out of Imperial policy. In 806 he was sent by Charlemagne on a mission to Pope Leo III. In 813 he was one of those who persuaded Charlemagne to crown his son Lewis the Pious as his co-emperor and heir. From his nickname Bezaleel and the fact

that Angisus worked under him at Aachen, it has been maintained that he must have had some responsible role in the
building of the cathedral and the royal palace in that town.[31]
That Einhard should not mention himself elsewhere in his
narrative is perhaps not surprising, in view of the fact that he
had written a personal introduction to the work. It remains
true that in Bk. III, §28, when he discusses the attack made
upon the Pope's person, he does not allude to the fact that he
had himself visited Leo III. When, in Bk. III, §30, the 'council
of the Frankish leaders' is convened and the decision made to
crown Lewis, Einhard could have referred to his own role in
this important event, but he fails to do so. Again in Bk. II,
§17, and Bk. III, §26, when he describes the building of the
cathedral at Aachen, and in Bk. III, §22, when he refers to the
construction of Charlemagne's palace, he makes no comment
on his own activities.

The brevity of *The Life of Charlemagne*, the clarity and the
general excellence of Einhard's Latin style compared with that
of the other German Latinists of the time and the neat and
satisfying way in which his biography is set out all bring us to
a new consideration. R. B. Mowat wrote of Einhard's 'genuine
literary talent'.[32] Louis Halphen has been equally admiring.[33]
The truth is that Einhard was following a model, or rather a
series of twelve models. It is known that a manuscript of the
De vita Caesarum of Suetonius existed in the library of the
monastery of Fulda at the time when Einhard studied there.
He had clearly read this work with great attention and his
Vita Caroli follows so closely the life of Augustus in particular,
both in form and in wording, that he may well have had a
transcription with him when he was writing his own work at
Seligenstadt, unless, as is possible, he knew much of Suetonius
by heart. As Louis Halphen writes, '*il l'a suivi si fidèlement, il a
repris en outre, à son tour, avec une telle servilité les expressions
familières à l'historien latin que sa Vie de Charlemagne apparaît
souvent plus comme la treizième "vie des Césars" que comme une*

oeuvre originale'.[34] Philipp Jaffé was one of the first to study
this debt in close detail. In the preface to his edition of the *Vita
Caroli,* he listed some thirty-two passages in which Einhard
owes clear debts either of subject matter or vocabulary to the
De vita Caesarum, no fewer than twenty of these being to the
life of Augustus.[35] To say that Einhard is following his models
so faithfully and with such slavish imitation that *The Life of
Charlemagne* is virtually a thirteenth chapter added to the
twelve which Suetonius left to us is perhaps an overstatement,
but in length, shape, sequence of material and even in expression there is undoubtedly a most striking similarity. This
in part explains the literary excellence of *The Life of Charlemagne*. It also explains certain weaknesses. We might have
hoped for something longer, but each of the twelve lives
written by Suetonius was one chapter only in a book. In each
of his *Lives* Suetonius follows a fixed pattern, and Einhard has
thought it necessary to arrange his material in the same rigid
way. Finally, in his portrayal of Charlemagne's character and
personal habits, Einhard painted a picture which is false in that
it resembles so closely those of the twelve Caesars. 'It is likely
enough that he was over-anxious to find resemblances between Charlemagne and Augustus where such resemblances
were either very remote, or even non-existent. His picture of
Charlemagne's habits and disposition, where it differs from
other pictures, seems to differ from them precisely in those
respects in which it agrees most with the Suetonian portrait of
Augustus.'[36]

    The Life of Charlemagne has been called 'the most striking
result of the Classical Renaissance so diligently fostered at the
court of Charlemagne by the Emperor himself',[37] and French
critics have maintained that as a biography there is nothing to
compare with it between the works of Suetonius himself and
Le livre des saintes paroles et des bonnes actions de Saint Louis by
Joinville. In his preface Einhard protests that he is 'but little
versed in the tongue of the Romans'. Modern critics, on the

contrary, see Alcuin and his contemporaries as 'mere fumblers and botchers' of Latin [38] when compared with Einhard. These are words of high praise and deep condemnation. Perhaps the safest conclusion for the reader of a modern translation, warned as he is against certain imperfections of subject matter and unaware as he must be of the excellence of Einhard's Latin style, is that of Louis Halphen who called Einhard's biography *'une oeuvre sans laquelle notre connaissance de la personne même de Charlemagne resterait bien incomplète'.*[39]

*

We possess eighty or more manuscripts of the *Vita Caroli*. Some sixty of these were used by G. H. Pertz in his monumental edition of 1829. In 1867 Philipp Jaffé abandoned the vast critical apparatus of Pertz and published a single manuscript, MS. Paris, Bibl. Nat., *fonds latin* 10758, copied in the ninth or tenth century. In 1880 appeared the edition of G. Waitz, who succeeded in reducing the eighty-odd extant manuscripts to three basic families and produced a critical version based upon twenty of them. This was revised by O. Holder-Egger in 1911. The editions published by H. W. Garrod and R. B. Mowat in 1915 and by Louis Halphen in 1938, 3rd edition 1947, are both based primarily on the Paris manuscript used by Jaffé and on MS. Vienna, Bibl. Pal. 510, with variants from other manuscripts.

This new translation is a rendering into modern English of MS. Paris, Bibl. Nat., *fonds latin* 10758, as published by Philipp Jaffé in 1867, some hundred years ago .

4. THE STAMMERING MONK OF SAINT GALL

About Einhard we know a surprising amount: it is probable that we have nearly as much information about the Monk of Saint Gall.

One piece of evidence which may or may not concern the

Monk must be recorded at the outset. The Benedictine monastery of Saint Gall, in the upland valley of the Steinach in the German–Swiss canton of St Gallen, included among its monks in the ninth and tenth centuries a series of at least four men called Notker: there was a writer, teacher and musician called Notker Balbulus, or Notker the Stammerer, born c. 840, who died in 912; another Notker became Abbot in 971 and died in 975; a physician, called Notker Piperis Granum, or Notker the Peppercorn, also died in 975; and a teacher and translator called Notker Labeo or Notker the Thick-lipped, died in 1022. As we shall see, the Monk of Saint Gall wrote his *De Carolo Magno* about 884. It contains one particularly striking passage, in which he describes the arrival in 773 of Charlemagne and his iron-clad army before the walls of Pavia to besiege Desiderius, King of the Longobards.[40] The description is strongly written, over ornate, laboured, extremely evocative, according to the taste of the reader. The author has certainly taken more care with it than with any other part of his narrative,[41] and there can be little doubt that he was pleased with what he had written. He ends with these self-deprecating words: '*Haec igitur, quae ego balbus et edentulus, non ut debui, circuitu tardiore diutius explicare temptavi* . . . – all this, which I, a toothless man with stammering speech, have tried to describe, not as I ought, but slowly and with labyrinthine phrase.' One may take this as a figure of speech, the literary conceit of a writer who concludes a purple passage, puts down his grey-goose quill, raises his face to a non-existent public and says to himself with disarming modesty, as he awaits a torrent of imagined applause: 'Poor stuff, this! I really haven't the talent which is needed! And, what is more, I am growing old!' On the other hand, one may take the passage literally: the author was less clear in his mind than he once had been, and rambled in his thoughts; he had lost his teeth and he suffered from a stammer. No doubt many of those who lived within the walls of the Benedictine monastery of Saint Gall in 884 had toothless gums. There could not have been so many stammerers. Perhaps there was only one: Notker Balbulus. In this case we have found our author. For the moment we shall be wise to reserve judgement.

To his *De Carolo Magno*, the Monk of Saint Gall wrote a preface. In Bk. I, §34, he tells us about it. The preface is lost; if we had it still, we should probably possess the secret of his identity. By reading his garrulous anecdotes carefully we can nevertheless assemble certain information about him. His native language was German,[42] and he came from the Thurgau,[43] to the south of Lake Constance and only a few miles from Saint Gall itself. He refers familiarly to the River Thur. As a child he was brought up by Adalbert, an old soldier, who had fought in the Carolingian wars against the Saxons, the Huns (= the Avars) and the Slavs, under the command of Kerold, one of the brothers of Charlemagne's Queen, Hildigard.[44] When the Monk was a small boy and Adalbert a very old man, the latter used to tell stories about his campaigns; and according to the Monk it is from his reminiscences that comes the description of the Avar state given in Bk. II, §1. Adalbert had a son called Werinbert, who became a Benedictine at Saint Gall and was probably responsible for finding a place for the Monk in that house. Werinbert was still alive when the Monk began to write his *De Carolo Magno*, and was one of the authorities mentioned in the lost preface. Just as the Monk reached the end of Book I, Werinbert died, on 30 May of an unspecified year.[45] The Monk includes himself among the 'sons and disciples' of Werinbert, but says that his own teacher was Grimald of Reichenau, according to him a pupil of Alcuin, who became Abbot of Saint Gall in 841 and died in 872.[46] In Bk. I, §10, he refers to Hartmut, 'then abbot of our house', and now a recluse in his cell.[47] The Monk mentions himself and his day-to-day existence in the monastery of Saint Gall on a number of occasions, either directly or indirectly. He says that he cannot be expected to visit Aachen and to prepare a word-picture of the cathedral built by Charlemagne because he is 'tied here' in his monastery.[48] Elsewhere he admits that he is a lazy man, 'more sluggish than a tortoise', and that he has never visited the land of the Franks.[49] His description of the monks rising for early-morning lauds, and often so overcome with sleep that they rest their heads on each other's shoulders, is obviously inspired from long personal experience.[50] Similarly, when Pepin the Hunchback, become, according to him, a monk at Saint Gall, sits on a rustic bench, surrounded by the older brethren, while the younger men are busy at more exacting occupations, and then takes a three-pronged hoe and digs away at the nettles and the weeds in the monastery garden, the Monk is no doubt describing things which he has often done himself.[51] Early in his book the Monk refers to one of the proudest possessions of his house, 'the reliquary filled with relics and made of solid gold studded with gems, which is called the Shrine of Charles'.[52] He is usually careful to stress the poverty of his monastery. He calls it one of 'the poorest and most austere of all places in the far-flung Empire'.[53] When he comes back into some measure of paternal favour, Pepin the Hunchback is only too quick to leave Saint Gall and move to Prüm.[54] The poverty and financial difficulties of the house, and the attempts of Abbot Hartmut, by appeals to Lewis the German and Charles the Fat, to have its affairs put on a more satisfactory basis are described in some detail.[55] The Monk mentions his monastery by name four more times: Charlemagne sent Peter the Cantor to Saint Gall, presented the house with an antiphonary and gifts of money and land, and gave the 'Shrine of Charles';[56] Tancho the Bell-founder had been a monk at Saint Gall;[57] Eishere, the warrior from the Thurgau, swears by Saint Gall,[58] presumably the Irish missionary rather than the monastery which he founded; and Stracholf the Glazier is a man from Saint Gall.[59] There are then the references to Charles the Fat, the epileptic great-grandson of Charlemagne, the youngest son of Lewis the

German, who was crowned Emperor in 881, became King of the East Franks in 882 and succeeded the West Frankish Kings, Lewis III and Carloman, in 882 and 883. On his way back from Italy, Charles the Fat visited Saint Gall for three days in 883.[60] 'I saw the King of the Franks, in full regalia, in the monastery of Saint Gall,' writes the Monk, and he then proceeds to give a description of the King's ceremonial dress which is hardly comprehensible: 'Two gold-petalled flowers stuck out from his thighs. The first of these rose up so high that it was as tall as the King himself; the second, growing gradually upwards, adorned the top of his trunk with great glory and protected him as he walked.'[61] If we still possessed the lost preface to the *De Carolo Magno* we should no doubt read that the book was presented to Charles the Fat. The Monk addresses him several times in the course of his narrative,[62] and the implication of the first of these personal statements is that Charles had asked for this book and stipulated that the anecdotes about bishops should be included.

Our author, then, is a German-speaking monk, who seems to have spent the whole of his adult life in the Benedictine monastery of Saint Gall. He began his *De Carolo Magno* in 883, or perhaps early in 884, and he brought the first book to an end in the first week of the June of this latter year, seven days after the death of Werinbert, a monk of his own house, who had provided him with some of his material. The second book follows straight on and was presumably started in the second half of 884; it was certainly finished before 11 November 887, when the Emperor Charles the Fat was deposed. Abbot Grimald was dead in 884; Abbot Hartmut had succeeded Grimald and then had retired to his cell. Whether the Monk's words '*balbus et edentulus*' are a figure of speech or a statement of fact matters little for the moment: if he really had lost his teeth, he was presumably no longer a young man. To have used the word '*edentulus*' at all, factually or figuratively, he must have reached the age when his teeth were worrying him,

or when their disappearance made eating and speaking difficult. If his description of horticultural activities in the monastery garden came from personal experience, and we see him
prodding the weeds with his hoe and then sitting back in the
sun on a rustic bench with the older brethren of the house, we
can again imagine him to be well into middle age.

Was the Monk of Saint Gall, a title given to him by modern
critics, really Notker the Stammerer? In his continuation of
Ratpert's chronicle of Saint Gall, the *Casus Sancti Galli*,[63]
Ekkehard IV (so called because there were three earlier monks
of some distinction with that same name in the monastery)
wrote of Notker the Stammerer that he was 'delicate of body
but not of mind, stuttering of tongue but not of intellect . . .'.[64]
Notker seems to have been born *c.* 840, at Jonschwyl on the
River Thur, just south of Wil. He died in 912. He was himself
teacher, poet, musician, chronicler, librarian and master of
guests. As Louis Halphen has made clear, the points of
similarity between the two writers are numerous:[65] both were
extremely interested in church music; both have a great pre-
dilection for the superlative forms of adjectives and adverbs,
and for the addition of diminutive endings to nouns and adjectives; certain peculiar idioms in Latin are common to them
both; their judgements of Julian the Apostate, Alcuin, Saint
Jerome and Saint Augustine are more or less identical, a circumstance which proves little; they are both greatly given to
quoting Virgil, which must have been a rare accomplishment
in 883–4. Finally, to set beside the quotation from Bk. II, §17,
of the *De Carolo Magno* which is given on p. 22, we possess
two different documents in which Notker describes himself
first as '. . . *balbus, edentulus et ideo blesus, vel, ut verius dicam,
semiblaterator* . . .'[66] and then as '. . . *jam edentulus, caeculus et
tremulus tam in superioribus quam inferioribus digitis* . . .'.[67] It is
clearly very probable that the Monk of Saint Gall who wrote
the *De Carolo Magno* really was Notker Balbulus. In what has
gone before I have preferred to leave the matter open, rather

than assume identity before I had explored the possibilities; and, despite the great probability that the Monk of Saint Gall and Notker the Stammerer were the same person, in the remainder of this book I shall continue to use the old non-committal title.

5. THE *DE CAROLO MAGNO* OF THE MONK OF SAINT GALL

When the *De Carolo Magno* is mentioned at all, it is customary to compare it adversely with Einhard's *Vita Caroli*. Philipp Jaffé began his very brief preface with these words: 'Since fiction is never far-removed from the history of human beings . . .' and went on to call the author of the *De Carolo Magno* 'a monk . . . who took pleasure in amusing anecdotes and witty tales, but who was ill-informed about the true march of historical events'.[68] A. J. Grant called the work of the Monk of Saint Gall a 'mass of legend, saga, invention, and reckless blundering'.[69] H. W. Garrod called it 'a largely mythical record'.[70] A. Kleinclausz was more sympathetic, but his conclusion was this: '*De quelque manière qu'on envisage la question, il reste acquis que le Charlemagne du moine de Saint-Gall est un Charlemagne de fantaisie et que ses Gestes, tels qu'il les rapporte, ont leur place marquée, non dans l'histoire vraie du fameux roi des Francs, mais dans son histoire légendaire.*'[71] As was his wont, Louis Halphen was strong in his condemnation: '*Nous ne croyons, pour notre part, ni à l'historicité ni à l'origine populaire de la légende propagée par le Moine de Saint-Gall.*'[72] All this is true. Our first danger is that when we put the *De Carolo Magno* side by side with the *Vita Caroli* we may be comparing it with something quite dissimilar; and our second that we may be criticizing both Einhard and the Monk of Saint Gall for failing to achieve what they did not set out to do. If we are committing one of these errors, or both, and they have become such commonplaces of literary criticism that one might say that they have been erected into a system, we may well obscure the value of what the Monk of Saint Gall has to offer to us. The historians of ancient Rome considered themselves free to write imaginary speeches for their historical characters, and to include or even to invent anecdotes about them; their account of events was subjective, literary, and often deliberately inaccurate; far from quoting precise references, the sources which they deigned to mention were more often than not false ones, and occasionally they were pure fabrications. Certain of these infuriating, if endearing, habits lasted down to Victorian times. As we have seen, there are many errors of fact, and some few deliberate ones of presentation, in Einhard's *The Life of Charlemagne*. We shall need even greater indulgence when we come to read the Monk's *Charlemagne*. Before we go any farther it may be wise to point out that if Alcuin 'was, moreover, a pupil of Bede', as is stated in Bk. I, §2, this is a remarkable thing, for the death of Bede and the birth of Alcuin both occurred in 735, or thereabouts; and that if, on the recommendation of the Monk, we go to Bede's *Ecclesiastical History* to find a whole book on Pepin the Short, we shall be gravely disappointed.[73]

The work of the Monk of Saint Gall has no title.[74] I have accepted the innocuous *De Carolo Magno* used by Philipp Jaffé, whose transcription of MS. Hanover XII, 858, I am following: this can only be translated as *Charlemagne*. It seems that the Monk set out to write a work divided into three books. The first of these books ends more or less with these words: 'Here I bring to an end my short treatise on the piety of our Lord Charlemagne and his care of the church . . .'[75] and this I have adopted as its title. In the same final chapter of his first book, the Monk goes on: 'The next book, which tells of the wars fought by the Emperor Charlemagne with such ferocity . . .'[76] and from this I have formed the title of Book II. We are apparently promised a third book, which shall describe Charlemagne's daily habits;[77] but this, like the book on Lewis the German mentioned in Bk. II, §11, was never written. As we have it, the *De Carolo Magno* is composed of two books: 'The piety of Charlemagne and his care of the Church' and 'The wars and military exploits of Charlemagne'. This is not a biography: and we must accept from the beginning that it will be very different from the *Vita Caroli* of Einhard, who was following so closely *The Lives of the Caesars* by Suetonius.

An analysis of the subject matter of the thirty-four chapters of Book I and the twenty-one chapters of Book II gives the following table, which immediately reveals what the Monk is doing:

Book I

§1. How Clement and a fellow Scottish missionary came to Charlemagne's court.

§2. How Alcuin the Englishman came to Charlemagne's court.

§3. The teaching of young boys at Charlemagne's court.

§4. *Anecdote 1:* How Charlemagne gave a bishopric to a provident young monk.

§5. *Anecdote 2:* The newly appointed bishop who, through gluttony, missed his place in the responses.

§6. *Anecdote 3:* The newly appointed bishop who leapt on to his horse.

§7. Reading and chanting in Charlemagne's chapel.

§8. *Anecdote 4:* How Charlemagne consoled the monk who could not sing.

§9. Alcuin and his pupils.

§10. Charlemagne and the Metz chant.

§11. *Anecdote 5:* The bishop who rebuked Charlemagne for eating early in the evening in Lent.

§12. *Anecdote 6:* The bishop who took the consecrated bread before offering it to Charlemagne.

Between the allegedly historical passages and the invented anecdotes the distinction is not always clear: to the anecdotes in Book II one might add, for example, the allegorical story of Pepin the Hunchback and the weeds in the monastery garden, or that of how Pepin the Short met the Devil, as he was on his way to take a bath in Aachen. If the list is left as it stands, in fifty-five chapters of unequal length there are twenty-eight historical passages and thirty-two anecdotes, the discrepancy being caused by the fact that certain chapters (Bk. II, §6; Bk. II, §7 and Bk. II, §21) contain more than one item.

I will consider the thirty-two anecdotes first. As many as seventeen are in some way critical of bishops, one is an attack on deacons, one is an attack on an unspecified cleric, and one deals harshly with lawyers. There is one kindly anecdote about a churchman, the story of the Bishop of Friuli on his death-bed. Four monks appear: two are rascals, and it is stated specifically that one of them comes from Saint Gall; with two we sympathize, and again it is made clear that one comes from Saint Gall. One anecdote makes fun of courtiers and one of ill-considered largesse at court. Two deal with brave soldiers, two with ambassadors and one with drunken young noblemen.

Secondly, the twenty-one attacks on bishops, monks, the deacon and the cleric are in Book I, 'The piety of Charlemagne and his care of the Church', and included here is the amusing story of the monk who could not sing. It would have been much neater to have moved over the Bishop of Friuli and Brother Stracholf, but the latter is a tale of Lewis the Pious.

Thirdly, the stories of brave soldiers, ambassadors, drunken young nobles, courtiers, lawyers and largesse are all in Book II, 'The wars and military exploits of Charlemagne', and the distinction is largely that they have nothing to do with the Church.

Fourthly, some twenty-four anecdotes are associated specifically with Charlemagne, three concern Lewis the Pious and five have no precise connexion with any of the Carolingian Emperors. It is obvious that the associations are arbitrary: little harm would be done if the anecdotes concerning Lewis the Pious and those where no Emperor is named were all ascribed to Charlemagne, or if those where Charlemagne appears were shared between Lewis the Pious and Lewis the German.

We are left with this conclusion: a very large part of the two books of the *De Carolo Magno* is nothing more than an anthology of monkish anecdotes, the '*iucundi narratiunculi salsaque dicta*' of Philipp Jaffé, the old familiar stories which succeeding generations of Benedictine brothers would tell and tell again, as age became more real for them and as they took their ease in the westering sunshine, warming their bones on the rustic seats in the monastery garden. They are mostly levelled at bishops, as one might expect from monks in their cloisters, and their author has a momentary anxiety on this score.[78] Their connexion with Charlemagne and Lewis the Pious is arbitrary and tenuous. They are harmless enough, and they usually have an obvious moral. One or two show a more daring touch. Of all this we can find later counterparts in the outside world: the *Gesta Romanorum*; the collections of stories in the French *romans à tiroir, Les Sept Sages de Rome* and its first sequel *Marques de Rome*, the former of which existed in so many languages before it came to France; the *fabliaux* collections of northern France in the twelfth and thirteenth centuries; Boccaccio; John Gower; and Chaucer.

Much more to our purpose are the twelve allegedly historical chapters in Book I and the sixteen in Book II. These are varied in the extreme. In Book I, six of the historical chapters deal rather cursorily with the revival of learning at Charlemagne's court, the so-called Carolingian Renaissance; two describe his building projects at Aachen, the cathedral and the imperial palace; and two touch lightly upon his distribution of benefices and his wars with the Huns (= the Avars), Slavs and Bulgars. Bk. I, §26, is a far more detailed description of the conspiracy against Pope Leo III, the arrival of Charlemagne in Rome and his coronation as Emperor on Christmas Day 800; but even here the Monk is anecdotal rather than historical in his treatment, and he certainly adds nothing to our knowledge. There remains the most interesting final chapter in the first book: how Charlemagne dressed in time of war. This description takes us back to Chapter 23 of Einhard's *Vita*

Caroli, and this time it is the Monk who is more detailed and precise. If Werinbert and his warrior father contributed anything to Book I, it is possibly this concluding chapter.

The sixteen historical chapters in Book II are for the most part even more anecdotal than the twelve in Book I. No fewer than seven of them consist of stories about Pepin the Short, Lewis the Pious and Lewis the German, not about Charlemagne at all. In four others we find tales connected with Charlemagne's diplomatic relations with Constantinople, Persia and a monarch whom the Monk calls vaguely the King of the Africans. In two we read anecdotal accounts of the coming to the valley of the Moselle of Godefrid, King of the Northmen, and of the piratical attacks of the Vikings in the south of France. The three chapters which remain are of much greater interest. They are spread evenly through the book. The Monk ends Bk. I, §34, by telling us how the old warrior Adalbert, who had fought against the Avars, Saxons and Slavs under the command of Kerold, brother of Queen Hildigard, used to tell him stories when he was a child.[79] The description of the lands of the Avars, with their nine concentric rings of fortification, each twenty feet wide, built up with logs, stones, heavy clay, sods of earth and living trees, and separated from each other by vast tracts of land, is presented as coming from Adalbert's reminiscences.[80] So is the story of Kerold's two brave captains,[81] although this is of little significance; and with these two passages one should read the description of Eishere, the warrior from the Thurgau.[82] This is living material and it is as arresting as anything in Einhard, but we shall be unwise if we accept much of it as reliable history. The story of the conspiracy of Pepin the Hunchback, the illegitimate son of Charlemagne, is mentioned briefly by Einhard.[83] The Monk adds much graphic detail about the plot itself, its discovery, the punishment of the conspirators, the enforced entry into the Church as a monk of the ringleader Pepin, his banishment to Saint Gall and his eventual move to

Prüm, called by him simply 'the most noble monastery then in existence'. Einhard, on the other hand, says nothing of Saint Gall, sends Pepin straight to 'the monastery of Prüm', and, anxious as ever to protect Charlemagne's memory, adds that Pepin went there to take up 'the life of a religious for which he had already expressed a vocation'. We may well hesitate to accept this localization at Saint Gall of part of the story; on the other hand, the Monk must have seen himself as writing primarily for the brethren of his own monastery, and he would not have introduced details which were not supported by local tradition, or, at least, could appear to be so if he stated them firmly enough. He then takes the opportunity to tell again, with considerable narrative skill, the story of Tarquin and the lilies, metamorphosed here into Pepin and the nettles.[84] The introduction of this age-old parable into the account of a historical event which took place in 785–6 is done in a way which cannot fail to puzzle the reader, for it is unlikely that Charlemagne, having been in danger of his life from Pepin and his fellow conspirators, would then, except in a mood of most sardonic paradox, ask this illegitimate son of his how he should treat a second gang of conspirators. However, once the Monk has started his story, he tells it with great realism and verve. The last of the three most striking chapters in the historical part of Book II is the remarkable description of the siege of Pavia in 773–4. If, in telling the story of Pepin the Hunchback, his three-pronged hoe and the nettles in the monastery garden at Saint Gall, the Monk shows how great his literary skill could have been if he had given it free rein, in the account of the siege of Pavia he composes a prose passage which is polished and self-conscious in the extreme. He imagines Desiderius, King of the Longobards, standing beside the fugitive Otker, on top of a watch-tower in Pavia. They peer northwards, across the Lombardy plain, and they look for the coming of their enemy. At length the Carolingian cavalry rides forward, wave upon wave, squadron after squadron, troop following troop. The fields bristle as with ears of iron corn. The sovereign's escort appears. Then comes in sight that man of iron, Charlemagne, topped with his iron helm, his fists in iron gloves, his iron chest and his Platonic shoulders clad in an iron cuirass. An iron spear raised high against the sky he grips in his left hand, while in his right he holds his still unconquered sword. . . . [85] This, in the Latin, is a piece of fine writing. According to our mood it reminds us of Sir Thomas Malory, Monk Lewis, Byron, Victor Hugo, William Morris. It cannot help but remind us of Lord Macaulay.[86] It should, instead, make us think of the French *chansons-de-geste*, for this man of iron, Charlemagne, topped with his iron helm, is soon to become the Charlemagne of the Old French epic:

> Par grant irur chevalchet li reis Charles,
> Desur sa brunie li gist sa blanche barbe.
> Puignent ad ait tuit li barun de France.[87]

Three things remain to be said about the *De Carolo Magno* of the Monk of Saint Gall. He is writing seventy years after the death of Charlemagne. What he offers is not a biography. He himself is very far from being an orthodox historian. His book lacks shape, and his Latin is far inferior to that of Einhard. It remains true, firstly, that, in some sense and in his own way, he is adding yet another chapter to the *De vita Caesarum* of Suetonius, less by direct imitation than by a familiarity with the work of Einhard, whom he never mentions. Careful reading soon reveals this. The Suetonian pattern is well known: ancestry and childhood; wars, as applicable; political and social activities; private life, character and domestic affairs; death, preceded by portents. In his inconsequential way, and with his thirty-two inserted anecdotes, the Monk can certainly not be said to be reproducing this plan. In the following table a selection of the events described by Einhard is set out, in the order in which they appear, and against them are placed the corresponding passages written by the Monk of Saint Gall:

This comparison is in some measure false, in that the data are selected and much is left out from each book: it remains striking in the extreme.

Secondly, the Monk of Saint Gall was in some measure a well-read man. His book is well larded with quotations from the Bible, mingled with more subtle references. Often they come in close sequence, e.g. in Bk. I, §33, Exodus, Joshua, Numbers, Matthew, Luke; or, at the end of Bk. II, §19, Galatians, Romans and Hebrews. He occasionally quotes from Virgil: *Aeneid*, III, 618; IV, 6; IV, 174–5; IV, 585; *Bucolics*, I, 63.[88] There is an inaccurate reference to Bede and a very trite one to Livy.[89] He sometimes borrows a word or two only, and one sees the reference by chance: '. . . *et per medios flammarum globos* . . .',[90] '. . . *instar militiae coelestis* . . .',[91] '. . . *cum ferrugine Hibera*'.[92] He quotes *The Life of Saint Ambrose* by Paulinus of Milan,[93] and makes two references to *The Life of Saint Martin* by Sulpicius Severus.[94] The debts to Einhard listed above are often textual as well as narrative. As shown in the notes he makes many twisted and ill-digested borrowings from the revised *Annales regni Francorum*, the Lorsch Annals and other similar texts.

There is a third point, which the reader may find hard to accept. Einhard knew Charlemagne intimately: he had been at his court for some twenty-three years. The Monk of Saint Gall, who had seen Charles the Fat for some three days only, was writing seventy years after the death of Charlemagne. Despite this, the Charlemagne of Einhard remains a stiff figure, a deified Roman Emperor, while the Charlemagne of the Monk of Saint Gall seems to live before our eyes and to be a little nearer to the real man whom we find portrayed elsewhere. He rounds in fury on the young noblemen who pay lip-service to learning and give little attention to the teaching of Clement.[95] When he is chiding his courtiers for their useless finery, he calls for his own rough jacket: 'Give that sheepskin of mine a rub between your fingers,' says he to his servant, as might Montgomery in the Western Desert, 'and then bring it in for me to look at.'[96] His condemnation of the short Gallic riding-cloaks is magnificently Wellingtonian: 'What is the use of these little napkins?' he asked. 'I can't cover myself with them in bed. When I am on horseback I can't protect myself from the wind and the rain. When I go off to empty my bowels, I catch cold because my backside is frozen.'[97] Maybe this is the jocular old Monk speaking, or maybe we are simply moving on from the Charlemagne of history towards the Charlemagne of romance.

*

The *De Carolo Magno* is found copied in with certain of the manuscripts which contain the *Vita Caroli* of Einhard. The edition of G. H. Pertz in *Monumenta Germaniae Historica, Scriptores*, Vol. II, pp. 726–63, Berlin, 1829, was based on a collation of these. The text of Philipp Jaffé, in *Bibliotheca Rerum Germanicarum*, Vol. IV, *Monumenta Carolina*, Berlin,

1867, reprinted 1964, which I have followed in this translation, is copied from Pertz, with variants from MSS Hanover XII, 858, Stuttgart *Theol. et Phil.* 4. IV. 242, and an unnumbered MS. once in the Abbey of Wiblingen.[98]

Willoughby Hall, Nottingham   LEWIS THORPE
31 December 1967

Full bibliographical details can be found in the Bibliography on pages 201–2.

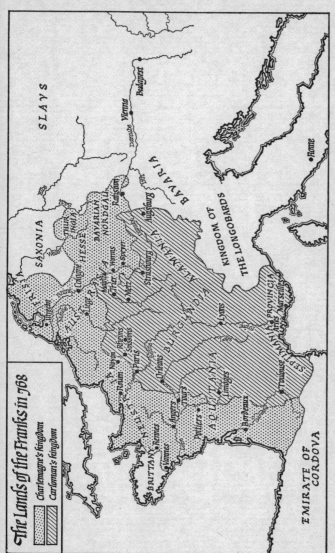

Map of the territory inherited by Charlemagne and Carloman in 768

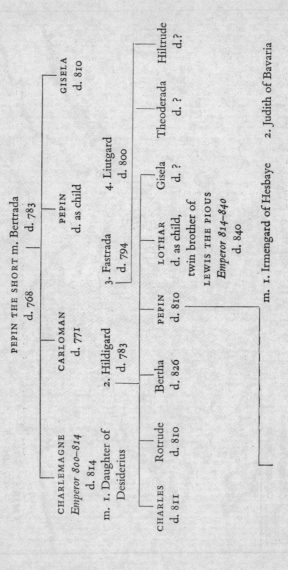

PEPIN THE SHORT m. Bertrada
d. 768

CHARLEMAGNE
Emperor 800–814
d. 814
m. 1. Daughter of
Desiderius

CARLOMAN
d. 771

PEPIN
d. as child

GISELA
d. 810

2. Hildigard
d. 783

3. Fastrada
d. 794

4. Liutgard
d. 800

CHARLES
d. 811

Rotrude
d. 810

Bertha
d. 826

PEPIN
d. 810

LOTHAR
d. as child,
twin brother of
LEWIS THE PIOUS
Emperor 814–840
d. 840

Gisela
d. ?

Theoderada
d. ?

Hiltrude
d. ?

m. 1. Irmengard of Hesbaye   2. Judith of Bavaria

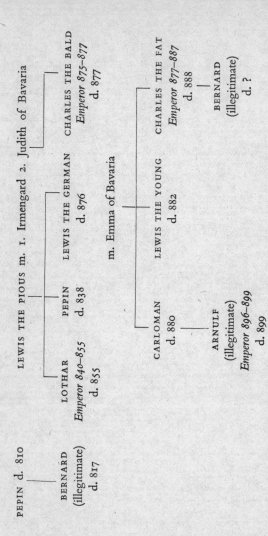

Genealogy of the Carolingians mentioned in the Two Lives of Charlemagne

THE LIFE OF CHARLEMAGNE

BY

EINHARD

WALAHFRID STRABO'S PROLOGUE

It is generally accepted that it was Einhard who wrote this life of the most glorious Emperor Charlemagne, together with the description of the historical events which form the background to the life. Einhard was one of the most highly thought of among all the palace officials of that time, not only for his knowledge of what really took place but also for his personal character, which was beyond reproach. He himself played a part in almost all the events which he described, so that he was really able to bring the strictest accuracy to his testimony.

Einhard was born in the eastern part of the Frankish dominions, in the district which is called the Maingau. As a boy he received his earliest education in the monastery of Fulda, in the school founded by Saint Boniface himself.[1] It was Baugolf, the abbot of the monastery of Fulda, who sent Einhard from there to the palace of Charlemagne. The reason for this was not Einhard's noble birth, although, indeed, he came from a distinguished family; it was because his talents and intelligence were most remarkable and that, even at so young an age, he gave great promise of the wisdom which was later to make him so famous. Of all kings Charlemagne was the most eager in his search for wise men and in his determination to provide them with living conditions in which they could pursue knowledge in all reasonable comfort. In this way Charlemagne was able to offer to the culture-less and, I might say, almost completely unenlightened territory of the realm which God had entrusted to him, a new enthusiasm for all human knowledge. In its earlier state of barbarousness, his kingdom had been hardly touched at all by any such zeal, but now it opened its eyes to God's illumination. In our own time the thirst for knowledge is disappearing again: the light of wisdom is less and less sought after and is now becoming rare again in most men's minds.

This tiny man, then – for Einhard's lack of inches was a great handicap to him – by reason of his wisdom and probity, achieved such fame at the court of Charlemagne, who was himself a greater seeker after knowledge, that among all the ministers of his royal Majesty there was hardly anyone to be found with whom the most mighty and sagacious King of his time was prepared to discuss more freely the secrets of his private affairs. There is no doubt at all that Einhard deserved this distinction: for not only in the time of Charlemagne himself, but under the Emperor Lewis the Pious, too – and this indeed is a miracle – when the Frankish state was shaken by innumerable troubles of all sorts and was falling to pieces in many areas, with God to watch over him and with a certain sense of direction in his personal conduct which can only have been divinely inspired, he preserved this reputation for brilliance which laid him open to the malice and ill-will of other men. What is more, he suffered no irremediable harm because of it.

All this I say so that nobody may have doubts about what Einhard has written, simply for want of knowing the man, the great debt of praise which he owed to the memory of his patron and the scrupulousness of the truth which he offered to the inquiring reader.

I, Walahfrid Strabo, have inscribed the headings[2] in this little work and made the chapter divisions as it seemed best to me, so that the reader may more easily consult any particular point in which he is interested.

EINHARD'S INTRODUCTION

Having once made up my mind to describe the life and the day-to-day habits of Charlemagne,[3] my lord and patron, and to write the public history of this most distinguished and deservedly most famous king, I have determined to be as succinct as possible. My aim has been to omit nothing relevant which has come to my notice and yet to avoid insulting the intelligence of fastidious readers by explaining at great length every fresh item of information. In this way my book may please even those who scorn the tales of antiquity as set down by the most competent and eloquent of historians.

I am sure that there are many men of leisure and learning who feel that the history of this present age should not be neglected and that the many events which are happening in our own lifetime should not be held unworthy of record and be permitted to sink into silence and oblivion. On the contrary, these men are so filled with a desire for immortality that they prefer, I know, to set out the noble deeds of their contemporaries in writings which may well have no great merit, rather than permit their own name and reputation to disappear from the memory of future generations by writing nothing at all. However that may be, I have decided that I myself should not refuse to write a book of this kind, for I am very conscious of the fact that no one can describe these events more accurately than I, for I was present when they took place and, as they say, I saw them with my own eyes. What is more, I cannot be absolutely sure that these happenings will in fact ever be described by anyone else. I have therefore decided that it would be better to record these events myself for the information of posterity, even though there is a chance that they may be repeated in other histories, rather than allow the extraordinary life of this most remarkable king, the greatest man of all those living in his own period, to sink into the shades of oblivion, together with his outstanding achievements, which can scarcely be matched by modern men.

Another reason had occurred to me and this, I think, not an irrational one. Even by itself it would have been sufficient to compel me to write what follows. I mean the care which Charlemagne took in my upbringing, and the friendly relations which I enjoyed with him and his children from the moment when I first began to live at his court.[4] By this friendship he bound me to him and made me his debtor both in life and in death. I should indeed seem ungrateful, and could rightly be condemned as such, if I so far forgot the benefits he conferred upon me as to pass over in silence the outstanding and most remarkable deeds of a man who was so kind to me, suffering him to remain unchronicled and unpraised, just as if he had never lived.

My own meagre talent, small and insignificant, nonexistent almost, is not equal to writing this life and setting it out in full. What was needed was the literary skill of a Cicero.

Here then you have a book which perpetuates the memory of the greatest and most distinguished of men. There is nothing to marvel at in it beyond Charlemagne's own deeds, except perhaps the fact that I, not a Roman by birth and a man but little versed in the tongue of the Romans, should have imagined that I could compose anything acceptable and suitable in the Latin language, and that I should have pushed my impudence so far as to scorn the advice given by Cicero in Book I of the *Tusculanae Disputationes*.[5] Speaking about Latin authors, he says there, as you can read for yourself: 'For a man to commit his thoughts to writing when he can neither arrange them nor bring any new light to bear upon them, and, indeed, when he has no attraction whatsoever to offer to his reader, is a senseless waste of time, and of paper, too.' This distinguished orator's advice would certainly have deterred me from writing, had I not made up my mind to risk being condemned by other men and endanger my own small reputation by setting these matters down, rather than preserve my reputation at the expense of the memory of so famous a man.

THE EARLY CAROLINGIANS

§1. The Merovingian dynasty, from which the Franks were accustomed to choose their Kings, is thought to have lasted down to King Childeric III, who was deposed on the order of Stephen II, the Pope of Rome.[6] His hair was cut short and he was shut up in a monastery. Though this dynasty may seem to have come to an end only with Childeric III, it had really lost all power years before and it no longer possessed anything at all of importance beyond the empty title of King. The wealth and the power of the kingdom were held tight in the hands of certain leading officials of the court, who were called the Mayors of the Palace, and on them supreme authority devolved. All that was left to the King was that, content with his royal title, he should sit on the throne, with his hair long and his beard flowing, and act the part of a ruler, giving audience to the ambassadors who arrived from foreign parts and then, when their time of departure came, charging them with answers which seemed to be of his own devising but in which he had in reality been coached or even directed. Beyond this empty title of King, and a precarious living wage which the Mayor of the Palace allowed him at his own discretion, the King possessed nothing at all of his own, except a single estate with an extremely small revenue, in which he had his dwelling and from which came the servants, few enough in number, who ministered to his wants and did him honour. Whenever he needed to travel, he went in a cart which was drawn in country style by yoked oxen, with a cowherd to drive them.[7] In this fashion he would go to the palace and to the general assembly of his people, which was held each year to settle the affairs of the kingdom, and in this fashion he would return home again. It was the Mayor of the Palace who took responsibility for the administration of the realm and all matters which had to be done or planned at home or abroad.

§2. At the time of Childeric III's deposition, Pepin the Short, the father of Charlemagne, was already performing this duty as if by hereditary right. Charles Martel, the father of Pepin the Short, had performed the same office with great success, inheriting it in his turn from his own father, Pepin of Herstal. It was Charles Martel who had crushed the despots who were claiming dominion for themselves throughout the whole land of the Franks. It was he, too, who had conquered the Saracens, when they were striving to occupy Gaul, in two battles, one in Aquitaine, near the city of Poitiers,[8] and the other by the River Berre, near Narbonne.[9] In this way he compelled them to withdraw into Spain.

It was customary for this title of Mayor of the Palace to be granted by the people only to those who outshone all others by family distinction and the extent of their wealth.

Pepin the Short, the father of Charlemagne, held the office for some years, under, if that is the word, King Childeric III, about whom I have told you. It had been handed down to him and his brother Carloman by their grandfather and their father, and Pepin shared it with his brother in the greatest harmony. Carloman then relinquished the heavy burden of administering a temporal kingdom and went off to Rome in search of peace, exactly for what reasons it is not known, but apparently because he was fired by a love of the contemplative life. He changed his dress, became a monk, built a monastery on Monte Soracte beside the church of Saint Sylvester, and there, in the company of the brethren who had come to join him for the same reason, enjoyed for some years the peace for which he longed. However, many noblemen from the land of the Franks kept journeying to Rome in the performance of their vows, as the custom is, and they were loath to miss visiting the man who had once been their lord. By their never-ending payment of respects they interrupted the calm which Carloman enjoyed so much and forced him to change his dwelling place. As soon as he realized that the perpetual repetition of this sort of thing must inevitably interfere with his plan, he left his mountain retreat and went off to the province of Samnium and the monastery of Saint Benedict on Monte Cassino, and there he passed in the religious life what remained of his earthly existence.[10]

§3. By the authority of the Pope of Rome, from being Mayor of the Palace Pepin was made King. He ruled alone over the Franks for fifteen years or more. Once he had finished the war in Aquitaine, which he had undertaken against Waifar, Duke of that country, and waged for nine consecutive years, Pepin died of dropsy in Paris.[11] Two sons survived him, Charlemagne and Carloman, and on these the succession of the kingship devolved by divine right. A general assembly was convened, according to custom, and the Franks appointed the two of them to be their Kings, on t he express condition that they should divide the whole kingdom equally, Charlemagne taking over the government of the part which their father Pepin had held and Carloman the part which their uncle Carloman had ruled.

These conditions were accepted on both sides and each received the half of the kingdom which had been allotted to him in this way. This harmony continued between them, but with great difficulty, for many of the partisans of Carloman did their best to break up the alliance, to the point that certain of them even plotted to engage the two in warfare. However, the course of events proved that this danger was more imaginary than real, for Carloman died, and his wife and sons, together with a number of men who had been the leaders among his nobles, fled to Italy. There, for no particular reason, except perhaps scorn for her husband's brother, the widow placed herself and her children with her, under the protection of Desiderius, King of the Longobards.

After having ruled the kingdom conjointly with Charlemagne for two years, Carloman died of some disease.[12] Once his brother was dead, Charlemagne was elected King with the consent of all the Franks.

BOOK II

THE WARS AND POLITICAL AFFAIRS
OF CHARLEMAGNE

§4. I consider that it would be foolish for me to write about Charlemagne's birth and childhood, or even about his boyhood, for nothing is set down in writing about this and nobody can be found still alive who claims to have any personal knowledge of these matters. I have therefore decided to leave out what is not really known and to move on to his deeds and habits and the other aspects of his life which need explanation and elaboration. First of all I shall describe his achievements at home and abroad, then his personal habits and enthusiasms, then the way in which he administered his kingdom and last of all his death, omitting from all this nothing which ought to be known or, indeed, which is worthy of being recorded.

§5. Of all the wars which Charlemagne waged, the first which he ever undertook was one against Aquitaine, which had been begun by his father but not brought to a proper conclusion. He thought that it would soon be over. He began it while his brother Carloman was still alive and even went so far as to ask his brother for help. Carloman did not give him the promised support; nevertheless Charlemagne pressed on energetically with the expedition which he had put into the field, refusing to withdraw from a campaign already started or to abandon a task once undertaken. In the end, with no small perseverance and continued effort, he brought to complete fruition what he was striving to achieve. After the death of Waifar,[13] Hunold had attempted to occupy Aquitaine and to renew a war which was almost over, but

Charlemagne forced him to evacuate the territory and flee to Gascony. Determined as he was not to let Hunold find refuge there, Charlemagne crossed the River Garonne and sent messengers to Lupus, Duke of the Gascons, to order him to surrender the fugitive. Charlemagne threatened to declare war on Lupus, too, if he did not do as he was ordered quickly. Lupus made a sensible decision: not only did he surrender Hunold, but he also submitted himself and the province over which he ruled to Charlemagne's suzerainty.

§6. Once matters were settled in Aquitaine and this particular war was finished, and now that his partner on the throne had been withdrawn from the anxieties of this world, Charlemagne next fought a war against the Longobards. He undertook this at the request of Hadrian, Bishop of the City of Rome, who first asked and then begged him to do so. This war, too, had been started in the first instance by Charlemagne's father, at the request of Pope Stephen, but in the most difficult circumstances, for certain of the Frankish leaders, whom Pepin the Short was accustomed to consult, were so opposed to his wishes that they openly announced their determination to desert their King and return home. Despite this Pepin declared war on King Haistulf and brought this war to a rapid completion. Although the reason for his undertaking the war was similar to that which had inspired his father, and indeed identical, it is clear that Charlemagne fought it with much more energy and brought it to a different conclusion. After besieging Pavia for a few days,[14] Pepin forced Haistulf to give hostages, to restore the towns and fortresses which he had taken from the Romans, and to swear an oath on the holy sacrament that he would not try to regain what he had surrendered. Once Charlemagne, on the other hand, had taken over the war, he did not stop until he had worn Desiderius down by a long siege and had received his surrender. He forced Adalgis, the son of Desiderius, on whom the hopes of everyone seemed to centre, to go into exile, not merely from his father's kingdom but indeed from Italy itself; he restored to the Romans everything which had been taken from them; he crushed a revolt started by Rotgaud, the Duke of Friuli,[15] subjected the whole of Italy to his own domination and made his son Pepin King of the territory which he had conquered. At this point I really should explain how difficult Charlemagne found the crossing of the Alps when he came to enter Italy, and after what effort on the part of the Franks the pathless ridges of the mountains were traversed, and the rocks which reared themselves up to the sky and the abrupt abysses; but in this present work I am determined to offer the modern reader a description of Charlemagne's way of life and not the day-to-day details of his wars. The outcome of this conflict was that Italy was subdued, King Desiderius was carried off into exile for the remainder of his life, his son Adalgis was expelled from Italy and everything stolen by the Longobard Kings was restored to Hadrian, the ruler of the Church of Rome.[16]

§7. Now that the war in Italy was over, the one against the Saxons, which had been interrupted for the time being, was taken up once more.[17] No war ever undertaken by the Frankish people was more prolonged, more full of atrocities or more demanding of effort. The Saxons, like almost all the peoples living in Germany, are ferocious by nature. They are much given to devil worship and they are hostile to our religion. They think it no dishonour to violate and transgress the laws of God and man. Hardly a day passed without some incident or other which was well calculated to break the peace. Our borders and theirs were contiguous and nearly everywhere in flat, open country, except, indeed, for a few places where great forests or mountain ranges interposed to separate the territories of the two peoples by a clear demarcation line. Murder, robbery and arson were of constant occurrence on both sides. In the end, the Franks were so irritated by these incidents that they decided that the time had come to abandon retaliatory measures and to undertake a full-scale war against these Saxons.

War was duly declared against them. It was waged for thirty-three long years and with immense hatred on both sides, but the losses of the Saxons were greater than those of the Franks. This war could have been brought to a more rapid conclusion, had it not been for the faithlessness of the Saxons. It is hard to say just how many times they were beaten and surrendered as suppliants to Charlemagne, promising to do all that was exacted from them, giving the hostages who were demanded, and this without delay, and receiving the ambassadors who were sent to them. Sometimes they were so cowed and reduced that they even promised to abandon their devil worship and submit willingly to the Christian faith; but, however ready they might seem from time to time to do all this, they were always prepared to break the promises they had made. I cannot really judge which of these two courses can be said to have come the more easily to the Saxons, for, since the very beginning of the war against them, hardly a year passed in which they did not vacillate between surrender and defiance.

However, the King's mettlesome spirit and his imperturbability, which remained as constant in adversity as in prosperity, were not to be quelled by their ever-changing tactics, or, indeed, to be wearied by a task which he had once undertaken. Not once did he allow anyone who had offended in this way to go unpunished. He took vengeance on them for their perfidy and meted out suitable punishment, either by means of an army which he led himself or by dispatching a force against them under the command of his counts. In the end, when all those who had been offering resistance had been utterly defeated and subjected to his power, he transported some ten thousand men, taken from among those who lived both on this side of the Elbe and across the river, and dispersed them in small groups, with their wives and children, in various parts of Gaul and Germany. At long last this war, which had dragged on for so many years, came to an end on conditions imposed by the King and accepted by the Saxons. These last were to give up their devil worship and the malpractices inherited from their forefathers; and then, once they had adopted the sacraments of the Christian faith and religion, they were to be united with the Franks and become one people with them.

§8. Despite the fact that it dragged on for so long, Charlemagne himself did not meet the enemy in fixed battle more than twice in the course of this war,[18] once near Mount Osning in a place called Detmold[19] and a second time on the River Haase.[20] These two battles were fought in the course of one month, with only a few days' interval between them. In them the enemy were so beaten and cowed that they never again dared to attack the King, or even to resist his advance, except when they were safe behind the earthwork of some fortified place. In this conflict there were destroyed many Frankish and Saxon nobles who held the highest positions in the state. Finally it came to an end only in its thirty-third year, although in the interim many other great wars had started up against the Franks in various parts of the world. These were directed by Charlemagne with such skill that anyone who studies them may well wonder which he ought to admire most, the King's endurance in time of travail, or his good fortune. This particular war against the Saxons began two years before the Italian campaign; and although Charlemagne pressed on with it unremittingly, no intermission was permitted in the wars being fought elsewhere, nor was a truce contemplated in any other military operation of comparable importance. Charlemagne was by far the most able and noble-spirited of all those who ruled over the nations in his time. He never withdrew from an enterprise which he had once begun and was determined to see through to the end, simply because of the labour involved; and danger never deterred him. Having learnt to endure and suffer each particular ineluctable circumstance, whatever its nature might be, he was never prepared to yield to adversity; and in times of prosperity he was never to be swayed by the false blandishments of fortune.

§9. At a time when this war against the Saxons was being waged constantly and with hardly an intermission at all, Charlemagne left garrisons at strategic points along the frontier and went off himself with the largest force he could muster to invade Spain. He marched over a pass across the Pyrenees, received the surrender of every single town and castle which he attacked and then came back with his army safe and sound, except for the fact that for a brief moment on the return journey, while he was in the Pyrenean mountain range itself, he was given a taste of Basque treachery. Dense forests, which stretch in all directions, make this a spot most suitable for setting ambushes. At a moment when Charlemagne's army was stretched out in a long column of march, as the nature of the local defiles forced it to be, these Basques, who had set their ambush on the very top of one of the mountains, came rushing down on the last part of the baggage train and the troops who were marching in support of the rearguard and so protecting the army which had gone on ahead.[21] The Basques forced them down into the valley beneath, joined battle with them and killed them to the last man. They then snatched up the baggage, and, protected as they were by the cover of darkness, which was just beginning to fall, scattered in all directions without losing a moment. In this feat the Basques were helped by the lightness of their arms and by the nature of the terrain in which the battle was fought. On the other hand, the heavy nature of their own equipment and the unevenness of the ground completely hampered the Franks in their resistance to the Basques. In this battle died Eggihard, who was in charge of the King's table, Anshelm, the Count of the Palace and Roland, Lord of the

Breton Marches, along with a great number of others. What is more, this assault could not be avenged there and then, for, once it was over, the enemy dispersed in such a way that no one knew where or among which people they could be found.

§10. Charlemagne also subdued the Bretons,[22] who lived along the Ocean shore towards the West, in one of the extremities of Gaul. They refused to obey his command, so he sent an expedition against them. As a result they were forced to give hostages and promise to do whatever he ordered them. Next he set out himself for Italy with an army, marched through Rome and advanced as far as Capua, a town in Campania. He pitched his camp there and threatened to declare war on the men of Benevento unless they capitulated.[23] Areghis, their Duke, prevented this, for he sent his two sons Rumold and Grimold to meet the King, with a large sum of money. He begged the King to accept his sons as hostages and promised that he and his people would obey Charlemagne's orders, with this one reservation that he should not be compelled to come in person. Charlemagne decided that it was more important to consider the interests of the people than to worry about their Duke's obstinacy. He received the hostages and as a great favour agreed that the Duke should not be forced to appear before him. He kept one of the two sons of Areghis, the younger, and dispatched the older one back to his father. He sent messengers to demand and receive oaths of fidelity from the Beneventans and from Areghis himself. Then he made his way back to Rome, spent some few days there in his personal devotions at the holy places, and so returned to Gaul.

§11. Next there suddenly broke out a war in Bavaria,[24] but this was very soon over. It was occasioned by the pride and folly of Duke Tassilo. He was encouraged by his wife, who was the daughter of King Desiderius and thought that through her husband she could revenge her father's exile,

to make an alliance with the Huns,[25] the neighbours of the
Bavarians to the East. Not only did Tassilo refuse to carry out
Charlemagne's orders, but he did his utmost to provoke the
King to war. Tassilo's arrogance was too much for the
spirited King of the Franks to stomach. Charlemagne summoned his levies from all sides and himself marched against
Bavaria with a huge army, coming to the River Lech, which
divides the Bavarians from the Germans. He pitched his camp
on the bank of this river. Before he invaded the province he
determined to discover the intentions of the Duke by sending
messengers to him. Tassilo realized that nothing could be
gained for himself or his people by his remaining stubborn.
He went in person to beg Charlemagne's forgiveness, handed
over the hostages who had been demanded, his own son
Theodo among them, and, what is more, swore an oath that
he would never again listen to anyone who might try to
persuade him to revolt against the King's authority. In this
way a war which had all the appearance of becoming very
serious was in the event brought to a swift conclusion. Tassilo
was summoned to the King's presence and was not allowed to
go back home afterwards.[26] The government of the province
over which he had ruled was entrusted from that moment
onwards not to a single duke but to a group of counts.

§12.   No sooner were these troubles over than Charlemagne
declared war on the Slavs, whom we are accustomed to call
Wiltzes, but whose real name, in their own language, is the
Welatabi. In this conflict the Saxons fought as allies alongside
certain other nations who followed Charlemagne's standards,
although their loyalty was feigned and far from sincere. The
cause of the war was that the Welatabi refused to obey
Charlemagne's orders and kept harassing with never-ending
invasions the Abodrites, who earlier on had been allied to the
Franks.

From the Western Ocean there stretches eastwards an arm
of the sea of unknown length, nowhere exceeding a hundred

miles in width, and, indeed, much narrower in many places.[27]
Round this sea live many peoples. The Danes and the Swedes,
whom we call the Northmen, occupy its northern shore and
all its islands. The Slavs, the Esthonians and various other
nations inhabit its eastern shore; and outstanding among these
are the Welatabi, against whom the King was now waging
war. A single campaign,[28] which Charlemagne directed himself, sufficed to crush and tame them, so that they never again
dreamed of disobeying his orders.

§13. The war which came next was the most important
which Charlemagne ever fought, except the one against the
Saxons: I mean the struggle with the Avars or Huns. He
waged it with more vigour than any of the others and with
much greater preparation. He himself led only one expedition
into Pannonia, the province which the Huns occupied at that
period. Everything else he entrusted to his son Pepin, to the
governors of his provinces and to his counts and legates. The
war was prosecuted with great vigour by these men and it
came to an end in its eighth year.[29]

Just how many battles were fought and how much blood
was shed is shown by the fact that Pannonia is now completely uninhabited and that the site of the Khan's palace is
now so deserted that no evidence remains that anyone ever
lived there. All the Hun nobility died in this war, all their
glory departed. All their wealth and their treasures assembled
over so many years were dispersed. The memory of man cannot recall any war against the Franks by which they were so
enriched and their material possessions so increased. These
Franks, who until then had seemed almost paupers, now discovered so much gold and silver in the palace and captured so
much precious booty in their battles, that it could rightly be
maintained that they had in all justice taken from the Huns
what these last had unjustly stolen from other nations.

Only two of the Frankish nobles died in this war: Eric,
Duke of Friuli,[30] who was surprised by an ambush of towns-

folk in Liburnia, near the maritime city of Tersatto; and
Gerold, the Governor of Bavaria, who was slain in Pannonia by an unknown hand, together with two men who
formed his sole escort when, just before a conflict with the
Huns, he was drawing up his line of battle and riding ahead to
encourage each of his troops by name. Otherwise this war was
almost bloodless as far as the Franks were concerned and its
outcome was most fortunate, although, because of its importance, it lasted so long.

Subsequently the Saxon war, too, ended in a settlement
which matched its drawn-out nature. Wars in Bohemia [31] and
Luneburg came next,[32] but they did not last long; they were
both brought to a swift conclusion under the direction of
the young Charles.

§14. The last war which Charlemagne undertook was
against those Northmen who are called Danes.[33] They first
came as pirates and then they ravaged the coasts of Gaul and
Germany with a large fleet. Their King Godefrid was so
puffed up with empty ambition that he planned to make
himself master of the whole of Germany. He had come to
look upon Frisia and Saxony as provinces belonging to him;
and he had already reduced the Abodrites, who were his
neighbours, to a state of subservience and made them pay him
tribute. Now he boasted that he would soon come with a
huge army to Aachen itself, where the King had his court.
There was no lack of people to believe his boasting, however
empty it really was. He was really considered to be on the
point of trying some such manoeuvre, and was only prevented
from doing so by the fact that he died suddenly. He was killed
by one of his own followers, so that his own life and the war
which he had started both came to a sudden end.

§15. These, then, are the wars which this powerful King
Charlemagne waged with such prudence and success in
various parts of the world throughout a period of forty-seven
years, that is during the whole of his reign. The Frankish

kingdom which he inherited from his father Pepin was already far-flung and powerful. By these wars of his he increased it to such an extent that he added to it almost as much again. Originally no more land was occupied by the Eastern Franks, as they were called, than the region of Gaul which lies between the Rhine, the Loire, the Atlantic Ocean and the sea round the Balearic Islands, together with the part of Germany which is situated between Saxony, the Danube, the Rhine and the Saal, which last river divides the Thuringians and the Sorabians. To this must be added, too, the fact that the Alamanni and the Bavarians formed part of the Frankish kingdom. By the campaigns which I have described, Charlemagne annexed Aquitaine,[34] Gascony, the whole mountain range of the Pyrenees and land stretching as far south as the River Ebro, which rises in Navarre, flows through the most fertile plains of Spain and then enters the Balearic Sea beneath the walls of the city of Tortosa.[35] He added the whole of Italy, which stretches for a thousand miles and more in length from Aosta to southern Calabria,[36] at the point where the frontiers between the Greeks and the men of Benevento are to be found. To this he joined Saxony, which forms a very considerable part of Germany and is considered to be twice as wide as the territory occupied by the Franks, while it is just about as long; then both provinces of Pannonia, the part of Dacia which is beyond the Danube, Istria, Liburnia and Dalmatia, with the exception of its maritime cities, which Charlemagne allowed the Emperor of Constantinople to keep, in view of his friendship with him and the treaty which he had made. Finally he tamed and forced to pay tribute all the wild and barbarous nations which inhabit Germany between the Rivers Rhine and Vistula, the Atlantic Ocean and the Danube, peoples who are almost identical in their language, although they differ greatly in habit and customs. Among these last the most notable are the Welatabi, the Sorabians, the Abodrites and the Bohemians, against all of whom he waged war; the others, by far the greater number, surrendered without a struggle.

§16. In addition to all this, Charlemagne made his reign more glorious by the friendly relations which he established with certain kings and peoples who became favourably inclined towards him. For example, Alfonso II, the King of Galicia and Asturias, became so close a friend that, when he had occasion to send letters or messengers to Charlemagne,[37] he ordered that he should always be called the King's own man. By the rich gifts which he gave them, Charlemagne had so influenced the Kings of the Irish that they never addressed him as anything else but their lord, and called themselves his slaves and subjects. There exist letters which they sent to him in which this subservience towards him is clearly shown.[38]

With Harun-al-Rachid, King of the Persians, who held almost the whole of the East in fee, always excepting India, Charlemagne was on such friendly terms that Harun valued his goodwill more than the approval of all the other kings and princes in the entire world, and considered that he alone was worthy of being honoured and propitiated with gifts.[39] When Charlemagne's messengers, whom he had sent with offerings to the most Holy Sepulchre of our Lord and Saviour and to the place of His resurrection, came to Harun and told him of their master's intention, he not only granted all that was asked but even went so far as to agree that this sacred scene of our redemption should be placed under Charlemagne's own jurisdiction. When the time came for these messengers to turn homewards, Harun sent some of his own men to accompany them and dispatched to Charlemagne costly gifts, which included robes, spices and other marvels of the lands of the Orient. A few years earlier Harun had sent Charlemagne the only elephant he possessed, simply because the Frankish King asked for it.

In the same way the Emperors of Constantinople, Nicephorus I, Michael I and Leo V, sought Charlemagne's friendship and alliance of their own free will, and sent many messengers to him.[40] When he accepted the title of Emperor, he aroused their strong suspicion, for he might well have been planning to take their own imperial power from them; but he concluded a firm treaty with them, in order to prevent any possible cause of dissension from arising between them. All the same, the power of the Franks always seemed suspect to the Greeks and Romans. Hence the Greek proverb which is still quoted today: If a Frank is your friend, then he is clearly not your neighbour.

§17. However much energy Charlemagne may have expended in enlarging his realm and conquering foreign nations, and despite all the time which he devoted to this preoccupation, he nevertheless set in hand many projects which aimed at making his kingdom more attractive and at increasing public utility. Some of these projects he completed. Outstanding among these, one might claim, are the great church of the Holy Mother of God at Aachen, which is a really remarkable construction, and the bridge over the Rhine at Mainz, which is five hundred feet long, this being the width of the river at that point. The bridge was burned down just one year before Charlemagne's death. He planned to rebuild it in stone instead of wood, but his death followed so quickly that the bridge could not be restored in time. He also began the construction of two magnificent palaces: one not far from the city of Mainz, near the township called Ingelheim; and the other at Nimeguen, on the River Waal, which flows along the southern shore of the Betuwa peninsula. More important still was the fact that he commanded the bishops and churchmen in whose care they were to restore sacred edifices which had fallen into ruin through their very antiquity, wherever he discovered them throughout the whole of his kingdom; and he instructed his representatives to see that these orders were carried out.

Charlemagne took upon himself the task of building a

fleet to ward off the attacks of the Northmen. For this purpose ships were constructed near to the rivers which flow out of Gaul and Germany into the North Sea. In view of the fact that these Northmen kept on attacking and pillaging the coast of Gaul and Germany, Charlemagne placed strongpoints and coastguard stations at all the ports and at the mouths of all rivers considered large enough for the entry of ships, so that the enemy could be bottled up by this military task force. He did the same in the south, along the shore of southern Gaul and Septimania, and along the whole coast of Italy as far north as Rome, against the Moors who had recently begun piratical attacks. The result of this measure was that during his lifetime no serious damage was done to Italy by the Moors, or to Gaul and Germany by the Northmen.[41] The only exceptions were Civitavecchia, a city in Etruria, which was captured and sacked by the Moors as the result of treachery; and certain islands in Frisia, near to the German coast, which were looted by the Northmen.

BOOK III

THE EMPEROR'S PRIVATE LIFE

§18. What has gone before is a fair picture of Charlemagne and all that he did to protect and enlarge his kingdom, and indeed to embellish it. I shall now speak of his intellectual qualities, his extraordinary strength of character, whether in prosperity or adversity, and all the other details of his personal and domestic life.

After the death of his father, at the time when he was sharing the kingship with Carloman, Charlemagne bore with such patience this latter's hatred and jealousy that everyone was surprised that he never lost his temper with his brother.

Then, at the bidding of his mother, he married the daughter of Desiderius, the King of the Longobards.[42] Nobody knows why, but he dismissed this wife after one year. Next he married Hildigard, a woman of most noble family, from the Swabian race. By her he had three sons, Charles, Pepin and Lewis, and the same number of daughters, Rotrude, Bertha and Gisela.[43] He had three more daughters, Theoderada, Hiltrude and Rothaide, two of these by his third wife, Fastrada, who was from the race of Eastern Franks or Germans,[44] and the last by a concubine whose name I cannot remember. Fastrada died and he married Liutgard, from the Alamanni, but she bore him no children.[45] After Liutgard's death, he took four concubines: Madelgard, who bore him a daughter Ruothilde; Gersvinda, of the Saxon race, by whom he had a daughter Adaltrude; Regina, who bore him Drogo[46] and Hugo;[47] and Adallinda, who became the mother of Theodoric.

Charlemagne's own mother, Bertrada, lived with him in

high honour to a very great age. He treated her with every respect and never had a cross word with her, except over the divorce of King Desiderius' daughter, whom he had married on her advice. Bertrada died soon after Hildigard,[48] living long enough to see three grandsons and as many granddaughters in her son's house. Charlemagne buried her with great honour in the church of Saint Denis, where his father lay.

He had a single sister, Gisela by name, who from her childhood onwards had been dedicated to the religious life.[49] He treated her with the same respect which he showed his mother. She died a few years before Charlemagne himself, in the nunnery where she had spent her life.

§19.   Charlemagne was determined to give his children, his daughters just as much as his sons, a proper training in the liberal arts which had formed the subject of his own studies. As soon as they were old enough he had his sons taught to ride in the Frankish fashion, to use arms and to hunt. He made his daughters learn to spin and weave wool, use the distaff and spindle, and acquire every womanly accomplishment, rather than fritter away their time in sheer idleness.

Of all his children he lost only two sons and one daughter prior to his own death.[50] These were his eldest son Charles,[51] Pepin whom he had made King of Italy,[52] and Rotrude, the eldest of his daughters, who had been engaged to Constantine, the Emperor of the Greeks.[53] Pepin left one son, called Bernard, and five daughters, Adelhaid, Atula, Gundrada, Berthaid and Theoderada. Charlemagne gave clear proof of the affection which he bore them all, for after the death of Pepin he ordered his grandson Bernard to succeed and he had his granddaughters brought up with his own girls. He bore the death of his two sons and his daughter with less fortitude than one would have expected, considering the strength of his character; for his emotions as a father, which were very deeply rooted, made him burst into tears.

When the death of Hadrian,[54] the Pope of Rome and his close friend, was announced to him, he wept as if he had lost a brother or a dearly loved son. He was firm and steady in his human relationships, developing friendship easily, keeping it up with care and doing everything he possibly could for anyone whom he had admitted to this degree of intimacy.

He paid such attention to the upbringing of his sons and daughters that he never sat down to table without them when he was at home, and never set out on a journey without taking them with him. His sons rode at his side and his daughters followed along behind. Hand-picked guards watched over them as they closed the line of march. These girls were extraordinarily beautiful and greatly loved by their father. It is a remarkable fact that, as a result of this, he kept them with him in his household until the very day of his death, instead of giving them in marriage to his own men or to foreigners, maintaining that he could not live without them. The consequence was that he had a number of unfortunate experiences,[55] he who had been so lucky in all else that he undertook. However, he shut his eyes to all that happened, as if no suspicion of any immoral conduct had ever reached him, or as if the rumour was without foundation.

§20. I did not mention with the others a son called Pepin who was born to Charlemagne by a concubine.[56] He was handsome enough, but a hunchback. At a moment when his father was wintering in Bavaria, soon after the beginning of his campaign against the Huns, this Pepin pretended to be ill and conspired with certain of the Frankish leaders who had won him over to their cause by pretending to offer him the kingship.[57] The plot was discovered and the conspirators were duly punished. Pepin was tonsured and permitted to take up, in the monastery of Prüm, the life of a religious for which he had already expressed a vocation.

Earlier on there had been another dangerous conspiracy against Charlemagne in Germany.[58] All the plotters were exiled, some having their eyes put out first, but the others were not maltreated physically. Only three of them were killed. These resisted arrest, drew their swords and started to defend themselves. They slaughtered a few men in the process and had to be destroyed themselves, as there was no other way of dealing with them.

The cruelty of Queen Fastrada is thought to have been the cause of both these conspiracies, since it was under her influence that Charlemagne seemed to have taken actions which were fundamentally opposed to his normal kindliness and good nature.[59] Throughout the remainder of his life he so won the love and favour of all his fellow human beings, both at home and abroad, that no one ever levelled against him the slightest charge of cruelty or injustice.

§21.   He loved foreigners and took great pains to make them welcome. So many visited him as a result that they were rightly held to be a burden not only to the palace, but to the entire realm. In his magnanimity he took no notice at all of this criticism, for he considered that his reputation for hospitality and the advantage of the good name which he acquired more than compensated for the great nuisance of their being there.

§22.   The Emperor was strong and well built.[60] He was tall in stature, but not excessively so, for his height was just seven times the length of his own feet. The top of his head was round, and his eyes were piercing and unusually large. His nose was slightly longer than normal, he had a fine head of white hair and his expression was gay and good-humoured. As a result, whether he was seated or standing, he always appeared masterful and dignified. His neck was short and rather thick, and his stomach a trifle too heavy, but the proportions of the rest of his body prevented one from noticing these blemishes. His step was firm and he was manly in all his movements. He spoke distinctly, but his voice was thin for a man of his physique. His health was good, except that he suffered from frequent attacks of fever during the last four years of his life, and towards the end he was lame in one foot. Even then he continued to do exactly as he wished, instead of following the advice of his doctors, whom he came positively to dislike after they advised him to stop eating the roast meat to which he was accustomed and to live on stewed dishes.

He spent much of his time on horseback and out hunting, which came naturally to him, for it would be difficult to find another race on earth who could equal the Franks in this activity. He took delight in steam-baths at the thermal springs, and loved to exercise himself in the water whenever he could. He was an extremely strong swimmer and in this sport no one could surpass him. It was for this reason that he built his palace at Aachen and remained continuously in residence there during the last years of his life and indeed until the moment of his death. He would invite not only his sons to bathe with him, but his nobles and friends as well, and occasionally even a crowd of his attendants and bodyguards, so that sometimes a hundred men or more would be in the water together.

§23. He wore the national dress of the Franks. Next to his skin he had a linen shirt and linen drawers; and then long hose and a tunic edged with silk. He wore shoes on his feet and bands of cloth wound round his legs. In winter he protected his chest and shoulders with a jerkin made of otter skins or ermine. He wrapped himself in a blue cloak and always had a sword strapped to his side, with a hilt and belt of gold or silver. Sometimes he would use a jewelled sword, but this was only on great feast days or when ambassadors came from foreign peoples. He hated the clothes of other countries, no matter how becoming they might be, and he would never consent to wear them. The only exception to this was one day in Rome when Pope Hadrian entreated him to put on a long tunic and a Greek mantle, and to wear shoes made in the Roman fashion; and then a second time, when Leo, Hadrian's successor, persuaded him to do the same thing. On feast days he walked in procession in a suit of cloth of gold, with jewelled shoes, his cloak fastened with a golden brooch and with a crown of gold and precious stones on his head. On ordinary days his dress differed hardly at all from that of the common people.

§24. He was moderate in his eating and drinking, and especially so in drinking; for he hated to see drunkenness in any man, and even more so in himself and his friends. All the same, he could not go long without food, and he often used to complain that fasting made him feel ill. He rarely gave banquets and these only on high feast days, but then he would invite a great number of guests. His main meal of the day was served in four courses, in addition to the roast meat which his hunters used to bring in on spits and which he enjoyed more than any other food. During his meal he would listen to a public reading or some other entertainment. Stories would be recited for him, or the doings of the ancients told again. He took great pleasure in the books of Saint Augustine and especially in those which are called *The City of God*.

He was so sparing in his use of wine and every other beverage that he rarely drank more than three times in the course of his dinner. In summer, after his midday meal, he would eat some fruit and take another drink; then he would remove his shoes and undress completely, just as he did at night, and rest for two or three hours. During the night he slept so lightly that he would wake four or five times and rise from his bed. When he was dressing and putting on his shoes he would invite his friends to come in. Moreover, if the Count of the Palace told him that there was some dispute which could not be settled without the Emperor's personal decision, he would order the disputants to be brought in there and then, hear the case as if he were sitting in tribunal and pronounce a judgement. If there was any official business to be transacted on that day, or any order to be given to one of his ministers, he would settle it at the same time.

§25. He spoke easily and fluently, and could express with great clarity whatever he had to say. He was not content with his own mother tongue, but took the trouble to learn foreign languages. He learnt Latin so well that he spoke it as fluently as his own tongue; but he understood Greek better than he could speak it. He was eloquent to the point of sometimes seeming almost garrulous.

He paid the greatest attention to the liberal arts; and he had great respect for men who taught them, bestowing high honours upon them. When he was learning the rules of grammar he received tuition from Peter the Deacon of Pisa, who by then was an old man, but for all other subjects he was taught by Alcuin, surnamed Albinus, another Deacon, a man of the Saxon race who came from Britain and was the most learned man anywhere to be found. Under him the Emperor spent much time and effort in studying rhetoric, dialectic and especially astrology. He applied himself to mathematics and traced the course of the stars with great attention and care. He also tried to learn to write. With this object in view he used to keep writing-tablets and notebooks under the pillows on his bed, so that he could try his hand at forming letters during his leisure moments; but, although he tried very hard, he had begun too late in life and he made little progress.

§26. Charlemagne practised the Christian religion with great devotion and piety, for he had been brought up in this faith since earliest childhood. This explains why he built a cathedral of such great beauty at Aachen, decorating it with gold and silver, with lamps, and with lattices and doors of solid bronze.[61] He was unable to find marble columns for his construction anywhere else, and so he had them brought from Rome and Ravenna.[62]

As long as his health lasted he went to church morning and

evening with great regularity, and also for early-morning Mass, and the late-night hours.[63] He took the greatest pains to ensure that all church ceremonies were performed with the utmost dignity, and he was always warning the sacristans to see that nothing sordid or dirty was brought into the building or left there. He donated so many sacred vessels made of gold and silver, and so many priestly vestments, that when service time came even those who opened and closed the doors, surely the humblest of all church dignitaries, had no need to perform their duties in their everyday clothes.

He made careful reforms in the way in which the psalms were chanted and the lessons read. He was himself quite an expert at both of these exercises, but he never read the lesson in public and he would sing only with the rest of the congregation and then in a low voice.

§27. He was most active in relieving the poor and in that form of really disinterested charity which the Greeks call *eleemosyna*. He gave alms not only in his own country and in the kingdom over which he reigned, but also across the sea in Syria, Egypt, Africa, Jerusalem, Alexandria and Carthage. Wherever he heard that Christians were living in want, he took pity on their poverty and sent them money regularly. It was, indeed, precisely for this reason that he sought the friendship of kings beyond the sea, for he hoped that some relief and alleviation might result for the Christians living under their domination.

Charlemagne cared more for the church of the holy Apostle Peter in Rome than for any other sacred and venerable place. He poured into its treasury a vast fortune in gold and silver coinage and in precious stones. He sent so many gifts to the Pope that it was impossible to keep count of them. Throughout the whole period of his reign nothing was ever nearer to his heart than that, by his own efforts and exertion, the city of Rome should regain its former proud position. His ambition was not merely that the church of Saint Peter

should remain safe and protected thanks to him,
means of his wealth it should be more richly adorn
dowed than any other church. However much he th
Rome, it still remains true that throughout his whole r   or
forty-seven years he went there only four times to fulfil his
vows and to offer up his prayers.[64]

§28. These were not the sole reasons for Charlemagne's
last visit to Rome. The truth is that the inhabitants of Rome
had violently attacked Pope Leo, putting out his eyes and
cutting off his tongue, and had forced him to flee to the King
for help.[65] Charlemagne really came to Rome to restore the
Church, which was in a very bad state indeed, but in the end he
spent the whole winter there. It was on this occasion that he
received the title of Emperor and Augustus. At first he was
far from wanting this. He made it clear that he would not
have entered the cathedral that day at all, although it was the
greatest of all the festivals of the Church, if he had known in
advance what the Pope was planning to do. Once he had
accepted the title, he endured with great patience the jealousy
of the so-called Roman Emperors, who were most indignant
at what had happened.[66] He overcame their hostility only by
the sheer strength of his personality, which was much more
powerful than theirs. He was for ever sending messengers to
them, and in his dispatches he called them his brothers.

§29. Now that he was Emperor, he discovered that there
were many defects in the legal system of his own people, for
the Franks have two separate codes of law which differ from
each other in many points.[67] He gave much thought to how
he could best fill the gaps, reconcile the discrepancies, correct
the errors and rewrite the laws which were ill-expressed.
None of this was ever finished; he added a few sections, but
even these remained incomplete. What he did do was to have
collected together and committed to writing the laws of all
the nations under his jurisdiction which still remained un-
recorded.

At the same time he directed that the age-old narrative poems, barbarous enough, it is true, in which were celebrated the warlike deeds of the kings of ancient times, should be written out and so preserved. He also began a grammar of his native tongue.[68]

He gave the months of the year suitable titles in his own tongue. Before his time the Franks had known some of these by Latin names and others by barbarian ones. He gave titles to the twelve winds, not more than four of which, if as many as that, had been distinguished before. To take the months first, he called January *wintarmanoth*,[69] February *hornung*,[70] March *lentzinmanoth*,[71] April *ostarmanoth*,[72] May *winnemanoth*,[73] June *brachmanoth*,[74] July *heuuimanoth*,[75] August *aranmanoth*,[76] September *witumanoth*,[77] October *windumemanoth*,[78] November *herbistmanoth*[79] and December *heilagmanoth*.[80] He gave the following names to the winds: the east wind he called *ostroniwint*, the south-east wind *ostsundroni*, the south-south-east wind *sundostroni* and the south wind *sundroni*; he called the south-south-west wind *sundwestroni*, the south-west wind *westsundroni*, the west wind *westroni*, the north-west wind *westnordroni*, the north-north-west wind *nordwestroni*, the north wind *nordroni*, the north-north-east wind *nordostroni* and the north-east wind *ostnordroni*.

BOOK IV

THE EMPEROR'S LAST YEARS
AND DEATH

§30. At the very end of his life, when old age and illness were already weighing heavily upon him, Charlemagne summoned to his presence Lewis, the King of Aquitaine, the only surviving son of Hildigard.[81] A council of the Frankish leaders was duly convened from the whole realm. With the agreement of all who attended, Charlemagne gave Lewis a half-share in his kingship and made him heir to the imperial title. He placed the crown on Lewis' head and ordered that he should be called Emperor and Augustus.[82] This decision of Charlemagne's was accepted with great enthusiasm by all who were there, for it seemed to have come to him as a divine inspiration for the welfare of the state. It increased Charlemagne's authority at home and at the same time it struck no small terror into the minds of foreign peoples.

Charlemagne then sent his son back to Aquitaine. He himself, although enfeebled by old age, went off hunting as usual,[83] but without moving far from his palace at Aachen. He passed what remained of the Autumn in this way and then returned to Aachen towards the beginning of November. While he was spending the Winter there, he was attacked by a sharp fever at some time in January and so took to his bed. As he always did when he had a temperature, he immediately cut down his diet, thinking that he could cure his fever by fasting, or at least alleviate it. He then developed a pain in the side, called pleurisy by the Greeks, in addition to the temperature. He continued his dieting, taking liquids as his only nourishment, and those at rare intervals. On the seventh day after he had taken to his bed he received Holy Communion, and then he died, at nine o'clock in the morning on 28 January, this being the seventy-second year of his life and the forty-seventh year of his reign.[84]

§31. His body was washed and prepared for burial in the usual way. It was then borne into the cathedral and interred there, amidst the great lamentation of the entire population. At first there had been some doubt as to where he should be buried, for he had given no directions about this during his lifetime. In the end it was agreed by all that no more suitable place could be found for his interment than the cathedral which he had built himself at his own expense in that town, for the love of God and of our Lord Jesus Christ, and in honour of His holy and ever-virgin Mother. He was buried there on the day of his death and a gilded arch with his statue and an inscription was raised above the tomb. The inscription ran as follows:

Beneath this stone lies the body
of Charles the Great, the Christian Emperor,
who greatly expanded the kingdom of the Franks
and reigned successfully for forty-seven years.
He died when more than seventy years old
in the eight hundred and fourteenth year
of our Lord,
in the seventh tax-year, on 28 January.[85]

§32. Many portents marked the approach of Charlemagne's death, so that not only other people but he himself could know that it was near.[86] In all three of the last years of his life there occurred repeatedly eclipses of both the sun and the moon; and a black-coloured spot was to be seen on the sun for seven days at a stretch. The immensely strong portico which he had constructed between his palace and the cathedral came crashing down to its very foundations one Ascension Day.[87] The wooden bridge across the Rhine near Mainz which he had built over a period of ten years, with such immense skill and labour that it seemed likely to last for ever, caught fire by accident and was burnt out in three hours, to the point that not a single plank remained, except what was under the water.[88] What is more, one day during the last expedition which he led into Saxony against Godefrid,[89] the King of the Danes, just before sunrise, as he was setting out from his camp and was beginning the day's march, he suddenly saw a meteor flash down from the heavens and pass across the clear sky from right to left with a great blaze of light. As everyone was staring at this portent and wondering what it meant, the horse which Charlemagne was riding suddenly lowered its head and fell, throwing him to the ground so violently that the buckle fastening his cloak was broken and his sword-belt torn away. He was picked up, without his arms and his cloak, by the attendants who were near and who ran to his aid. Even his javelin, which he was holding tightly in his hand, fell from his grasp and lay twenty feet or more away from him.

There were frequent earth-tremors in the palace at Aachen; and in the apartments where Charlemagne lived the wooden beams of the ceiling kept on creaking. The cathedral in which he was subsequently buried was struck by lightning and the golden apple which adorned the highest point of the roof was dashed off by a thunderbolt and thrown on the top of the Bishop's house, which was next door. In the cathedral itself, along the edge of the horizontal ribs which ran right round the interior of the building and divided the upper arches from those on ground level, there was written in red ochre an inscription which recorded the name of the man who had constructed it. The words *Karolus Princeps* were included in the first phrase. In the very year of Charlemagne's death, only a few months before he died, people noticed that the lettering of the word *Princeps* was beginning to fade and that it eventually became illegible.

Charlemagne took no notice at all of these portents; or at least he refused to admit that any of them could have any connexion with his own affairs.

BOOK V

CHARLEMAGNE'S LAST WILL
AND TESTAMENT

§33. Charlemagne resolved to draw up a will by which he could make his daughters, and the sons whom his concubines had borne him, heirs to some part of his property. He began this too late, however, and it was never finished. Three years before his death he shared out his treasures, his money, his clothes and his furniture, in the presence of his friends and ministers. He instructed them to make absolutely sure that the division which he had planned should be put into effect after his death. He had a statement prepared to show just what he wanted done with the objects which he had shared out.

The text of this document ran as follows:

In the name of the Lord God Almighty, the Father, the Son and the Holy Ghost. This catalogue of his possessions and these suggestions for their disposal have been drawn up by Charles, the august, most pious and most glorious Lord and Emperor, in the eight hundred and eleventh year after the Incarnation of our Lord Jesus Christ, the forty-third year of Charlemagne's reign over the land of the Franks, in the thirty-sixth year of his reign over Italy, in the eleventh year of his being Emperor and in the fourth tax year.

With pious and prudent forethought he has resolved to make this partition of his valuables and of the moneys which were stored up in his treasure-house on that particular day, and with God's help he has proceeded to do so. His essential objects in planning this division have been to ensure that the distribution of alms which from long tradition Christians offer from their personal effects should be made methodically and sensibly from his own fortune, too; and then that his heirs should know clearly and without any possible misunderstanding what ought to come to each of them and so should be able to divide his possessions among themselves without lawsuit or dissension, each receiving his allotted share.

With this intention and object in mind, he has first of all divided into three parts all the valuables and precious objects which were to be found in his treasure-house in the form of gold, silver, jewels and regalia on the day stipulated. The first third he has placed on one side. The remaining two thirds he has subdivided into twenty-one parts. This division of the two thirds into twenty-one parts has been made for the following reason. It is well known that there are twenty-one metropolitan cities in Charlemagne's kingdom. Each of these parts shall be handed by his heirs and friends to one of these cities to be used for charity. The Archbishop who at the time of Charlemagne's death is in charge of each of the sees in question shall receive the part allocated to his own diocese. He shall share it with his suffragans in the following way: one third shall go to his own church and the remaining two thirds shall be divided among the suffragans. Each of these subdivisions, which have been made from the aforesaid two thirds, according to the recognized number of twenty-one metropolitan cities, lies in its own coffer, separated systematically from the others and with the name of the city to which it is destined written clearly on it. The names of the metropolitan cities to which these alms or *eleemosyna* are to go are as follows: Rome, Ravenna, Milan, Cividale, Grado, Cologne, Mainz, Juvavum or Salzburg, Trier, Sens, Besançon, Lyons, Rouen, Rheims, Arles, Vienne, Moutiers-en-Tarantaise, Embrun, Bordeaux, Tours and Bourges.

The following use shall be made of the third which Charlemagne has decided to keep intact. When the other two thirds have been divided up in the way stated and have been stored away under seal, the remaining third, which has not been alienated from his personal possession by any bond, shall be used for day-to-day expenses. It shall be so used as long as he remains alive or judges that he still has need of it. After his death or his voluntary withdrawal from the affairs of this world it shall be split up into four subdivisions. One of these quarters shall be added to the twenty-one shares already mentioned. The second quarter, destined for his own sons and daughters, and for the sons and daughters of his sons, shall be divided between them in a just and reasonable manner. The third quarter shall be devoted to the use of the poor, as is the custom among Christians. In the same way, the fourth quarter shall be shared out and shall come as a pension, in the name of Christian charity, to the servants, both men and women, who perform their duties in the royal palace.

Charlemagne has decreed that to this third part of his total fortune which, like the other two thirds, is composed of gold and silver, shall be added all the vessels and utensils of bronze, iron and other metals, together with his arms, clothes and all other movable objects, whether of value or not, and for whatsoever use they are put, such as curtains, bedcovers, tapestries, woollen stuffs, skins, harnesses and all else which happened to be found in his treasure-house and his wardrobe on that particular day, so that the subdivisions of that third part may be larger and the distribution of alms find its way to a greater number of people.

He has ordered that his chapel, that is to say the furnishings of his church, including both what he has himself given and collected together and what has come to him by inheritance from his father, should remain intact and should not be split up in any way. If, however, any vessels, books or other equipment are found there which have most clearly not been given by him to the chapel, then these may be purchased and owned by anyone who wishes to have them, providing that they pay a reasonable price. In the same way he has decreed that the great collection of books which he has made in his library shall be bought at a reasonable price by anybody who wants to have them, and the money given to the poor.

Among his other treasures and property there are three tables made of silver and a particularly big and heavy one made of gold. He has made the following decisions and decrees about these. The first table, which is square in shape and on which is traced a map of the city of Constantinople, shall be sent to Rome to the cathedral of the blessed Apostle Peter, along with the other gifts which are set aside for that purpose. The second table, which is circular, and which is engraved with a map of the city of Rome, shall be dispatched to the bishopric of the church of Ravenna. The third, which is far superior to the others, both in the beauty of its workmanship and in weight, and on which is engraved in fine and delicate tracery a design which shows the entire universe in three concentric circles, shall be added to that third part which is to be divided among his heirs and those who receive alms. With it shall go the golden table, which is listed as the fourth one.

Charlemagne has drawn up this catalogue and partition of his goods in the presence of the following bishops, abbots and counts who were able to attend. Their names are set out in the following list:

Bishops: Hildebald,[90] Richolf,[91] Arn,[92] Wolfar,[93] Bernoin,[94] Laidrad,[95] John,[96] Theodulf,[97] Jesse,[98] Heito,[99] Waltgaud.[100]
Abbots: Fridugis,[101] Adalung,[102] Engilbert,[103] Irmino.[104]
Counts: Walah,[105] Meginher,[106] Otulf,[107] Stephen,[108] Unruoc,[109] Burchard,[110] Meginhard,[111] Hatto, Rihwin,[112] Edo,[113] Ercangar, Gerold,[114] Bero,[115] Hildigern, Hroccolf.

Charlemagne's son Lewis, who succeeded him by divine right, read this statement and acted upon it with complete scrupulousness as soon as he possibly could after his father's death.[116]

CHARLEMAGNE

BY

NOTKER THE STAMMERER

MONK OF SAINT GALL

BOOK I

THE PIETY OF CHARLEMAGNE AND
HIS CARE OF THE CHURCH

§1.   He who ordains the fate of kingdoms and the march of the centuries, the all-powerful Disposer of events, having destroyed one extraordinary image, that of the Romans, which had, it was true, feet of iron, or even feet of clay, then raised up, among the Franks, the golden head of a second image, equally remarkable, in the person of the illustrious Charlemagne.

At the moment when Charlemagne had begun to reign as sole King in the western regions of the world,[1] two Scots from Ireland happened to visit the coast of Gaul in the company of some British traders.[2] These men were unrivalled in their knowledge of sacred and profane letters, at a time when the pursuit of learning was almost forgotten throughout the length and breadth of Charlemagne's kingdom and the worship of the true God was at a very low ebb. They had nothing on display to sell, but every day they used to shout to the crowds who had collected together to buy things: 'If anyone wants some wisdom, let him come to us and receive it: for it is wisdom which we have for sale.' They announced that they wanted to sell wisdom because they saw that the people were more interested in what had to be paid for than in anything given free. Either they really thought that they could persuade the crowds who were buying other things to pay for wisdom, too; or else, as subsequent events proved to be true, they hoped that by making this announcement they would become a source of wonder and astonishment. They went on shouting their wares in public so long that in the end the news was carried by the onlookers, who certainly found them remarkable and maybe thought them wrong in the head, to the ears of King Charlemagne himself, who was always an admirer and a great collector of wisdom. He ordered them to be summoned to his presence immediately; and he asked them if it was true, as everyone was saying, that they had brought wisdom with them. They answered: 'Yes, indeed, we have it: and, in the name of God, we are prepared to impart it to any worthy folk who seek it.' When Charlemagne asked them what payment they wanted for wisdom, they answered: 'We make no charge, King. All we ask is a place suitable for us to teach in and talented minds to train; in addition, of course, to food to eat and clothes to wear, for without these our mission cannot be accomplished.' Charlemagne was delighted to receive this answer. For a short time he kept them both with him. Later on, when he was obliged to set out on a series of military expeditions, he established one of the two, who was called Clement, in Gaul itself. In his care he placed a great number of boys chosen not only from the noblest families but also from middle-class and poor homes; and he made sure that food should be provided and that accommodation suitable for study should be made available. Charlemagne sent the second man to Italy and put him in charge of the monastery of Saint Augustine, near the town of Pavia, so that all who wished might join him there and receive instruction from him.[3]

§2. A certain Alcuin, an Englishman, heard that the holy Emperor Charlemagne was keen to welcome men of learning; he put to sea and came to meet the Emperor.[4] Alcuin, a man more skilled in all branches of knowledge than any other person of modern times, was, moreover, a pupil of Bede,[5] that priest of great learning, himself the most accomplished interpreter of the Scriptures since Saint Gregory.[6] Charlemagne received Alcuin with great kindness and kept him close at his side as long as he lived, except on the frequent occasions when he set out with his armies on mighty wars. The Emperor went so far as to have himself called Alcuin's pupil, and to call Alcuin his master. He gave Alcuin the rule of the Abbey of Saint Martin, near the city of Tours, so that, when he himself was away, Alcuin could rest there and continue to instruct all those who flocked to him. His teaching bore such fruit among his pupils that the modern Gauls or Franks came to equal the Romans and the Athenians.

§3. When, after a long absence, Charlemagne returned to Gaul, with a long series of victories to his credit, he ordered the boys whom he had entrusted to Clement's care to visit him and present to him their prose writings and their poems. Those of middle-class parentage and from very poor homes brought excellent compositions, adorned more than he could even have hoped with all the subtle refinements of knowledge; but the children of noble parents presented work which was poor and full of stupidity. Then Charlemagne, imitating in his great wisdom the justice of the eternal Judge, placed those who had worked well on his right hand and said to them: 'My children, I am grateful to you, for you have tried your very hardest to carry out my commands and to learn everything which will be of use to you. Continue to study hard and to strive for perfection; and I will give you bishoprics and fine monasteries, and you will always be honoured in my sight.' Then he turned with great severity to those on his left, with a frown and a fiery glance which seemed to pierce their consciences, and scornfully thundered out these frightening words: 'But you young nobles, you, the pleasure-loving and dandified sons of my leaders, who trust in your high birth and your wealth, and care not a straw for my command or for your own advancement, you have neglected the pursuit of learning and have indulged yourselves in time-wasting follies and in the childish sport of fine living and idleness.' When he had said this, he turned his august head and raised his unconquered right hand towards the heavens, and thundered forth an oath against them: 'By the King of Heaven, I think nothing of your nobility and your fine looks! Others can admire you for these things if they wish! Know this for certain, unless you immediately make up for your previous idleness by diligent study, you will never receive anything worth having from Charlemagne!'

§4. From among the poor lads whom I have described Charlemagne transferred to his own chapel one who was especially good at reading and writing. This name of chapel the Kings of the Franks used to give to their own private oratory, from the *cappa* or cope of Saint Martin, which they always carried with them in battle, both for their own protection and for the confounding of their enemies.[7] One day it was announced to our provident King Charlemagne that a certain bishop had died. He asked if, from his possessions, the bishop had left anything for the good of his own soul. The messenger replied: 'My Lord, no more than two pounds of silver.' At this the young man whom I have mentioned gave a sigh. Unable to keep to himself the thought which flashed through his mind, he said, with the King listening: 'A small provision for a journey which is long and never-ending!' Charlemagne, who was the most self-controlled of men, thought this over for a while and then said to the young man: 'Do you think, then, if you were to receive this bishopric, that you would take care to set more aside for the long journey?' The young man swallowed these cautious words as if they were the first ripe grapes of the season falling into the mouth of one agape for them. He fell at the feet of Charlemagne and said: 'My Lord, it depends upon the will of God and your own decision.' 'Stand behind this curtain, which hangs at my back,' replied the King, 'and hear how many sponsors you will have for this honour.' When the officials of the palace, who were always on the watch for the mishaps or even deaths of others, heard that this particular bishop was dead, they all began to canvass their own claims to the bishopric through those in the close confidence of the Emperor, showing impatience at the delay and jealousy of each other. The Emperor, for his part, persisted in his plan and was not prepared to change his mind; he refused the bishopric to everyone and said he would not break his promise to the young man.

In the end Queen Hildigard sent some of the nobles of the kingdom to the King and then actually came herself to beg the bishopric for one of her own clerics. The King listened politely to her request. He said that he would not and could not refuse her anything, but he was not willing to let down his own little churchman. It is the way of all women to want their own particular plan and solution to take preference over the decisions made by their menfolk; and so the Queen concealed the anger which was rising in her heart, lowered her firm voice to a whisper and tried to sway the Emperor's resolute mind with her soft caresses. 'My Lord King,' she said, 'what can it possibly matter if this young man of yours does not receive the bishopric? I beg of you, my sweet Lord, you who are my refuge and my glory, give it instead to my own cleric, who after all is a faithful servant of yours, too.' At this the young man, whom the King had ordered to stand behind the curtain near to which he was himself seated, so that he could overhear the way in which all the other candidates in turn presented their case, put his arms round the King, curtain and all, and interrupted the petitions. 'Hold firm, my Lord King!' said he. 'Do not let anyone snatch from your hands the power which has been given to you by God!' The King, who was a great believer in frank behaviour, called him out into the open and said to him: 'I am determined that you shall have this bishopric; but take care that you put on one side greater provisions and more expenses for the long inevitable journey which lies before you, and before me, too.'

§5. At the King's court there was a certain cleric who was mean and humble and not even very good at his studies.

Charlemagne, who was most kind-hearted, took pity on his poverty. Although everyone disliked him and wanted to get rid of him, he refused to dismiss the man or banish him from his presence, despite all the persuasion which was brought to bear on him. It happened one Saint Martin's Eve that the death of a certain bishop was announced to the Emperor. He summoned one of his clerics, who was well known for his ability and erudition, and presented the bishopric to him. The man was so overjoyed that he forgot himself. He invited to his own home a great number of the officials of the palace; at the same time he received with immense pomp a crowd of people who had arrived from his diocese; and to all these folk he offered a magnificent feast. Heavy with food, drowned in drink and more than half asleep from the wine which he had consumed, he then chose that most holy of nights to fail to turn up at the nocturnal vigil. It was, of course, the custom that earlier in the day the choir-master allocated to all those who were to be present the response which they should chant at night. To this individual, who now held a bishopric in his hand, the response allocated was 'Domine, si adhuc populo tuo sum necessarius'.[8] He was not in his place; and after the lesson there ensued a long silence. All those present urged each other on to chant the response, but everyone answered that it was his duty to chant only the response which had been assigned to him. At last the Emperor said: 'Come, come, one of you must chant it!' It was the mean and humble monk, strengthened by the will of God and encouraged by the King's direct command, who took up the response. The kindly King, who had little hope that he would know it well enough to be able to sing it right through, soon ordered the others to help him out. Immediately they all began to chant, but he, poor creature, hadn't the wit to pick up the line. When the response should have come to an end, he went on to chant the Lord's Prayer, with, it is true, the correct intoning. All the others wanted to stop him making such a mess of things; but in his great wisdom Charlemagne forbade anyone to interfere with him, for he wished to see how far he would go. He finished his verse with the words '*Adveniat regnum tuum*'; and all the others, willy-nilly, were then forced to give the response '*Fiat voluntas tua*'.

When early-morning lauds were over, the King returned to his palace, or more precisely to his heated bedroom, to warm himself up and to put on suitable clothes in honour of the coming Saint's Day. He ordered his humble servant, the new cantor, to come to him. 'Whoever told you to sing that response?' he demanded. The man was petrified with fear, but he answered, 'My Lord, you gave the order that someone must sing.' The King again asked – for King was the title which was used by our ancestors for the ruler of the Empire – 'But who picked that particular verse for you, out of all the others?' Inspired, so it is thought, by the spirit of God, the man then mumbled the following words, with which, at that time, superiors used to be honoured, flattered or even fawned upon by their inferiors: 'Blessed Lord, beneficent King, when I could not discover the correct verse from any-one, I said in my heart that I should incur your Majesty's displeasure if I introduced anything odd. I therefore decided to intone the verse the last words of which usually come at the end of the response.'

The Emperor, who was most moderate in all his ways, smiled gently at him, and then announced in the presence of his nobles: 'That proud man had so little respect or honour for his God, or for the King who had befriended him, that he could not refrain from dissipation just for one night, so that he might at least be present to start off the response which, so I hear, he was supposed to sing. He must therefore forfeit his bishopric, by God's decree and my own. You take on the responsibility of administering it instead, for God gives it to you, and I agree, but try to do it according to the canonical and apostolic rule.'

§6. On the occasion of the death of another bishop, the Emperor appointed a young man in his place. When he emerged rejoicing and ready to start on his journey, his servants, in recognition of his episcopal status, led out his horse and placed steps so that he could climb up. He took it amiss that they should treat him as if he were infirm, and leapt on the horse from the ground, with the result that he had difficulty in holding on without falling off again on the other side. The King observed this from the balustrade of his palace, immediately ordered him to be called back and spoke to him as follows: 'My good man, you are quick and agile, nimble and active. You know very well that the peace of our empire is disturbed on all sides by a veritable maelstrom of innumerable wars. I obviously need such a churchman as you in my immediate entourage. You had better stay behind here to share my labours, seeing that you can leap on a horse with such agility.'

§7. When I was describing the allocation of the responses, I forgot to mention the arrangement made for public reading, and I must devote a few words to that subject here. There was never anyone present in the cathedral of the most learned Charlemagne to remind each reader which passages should be recited; and when he reached the end of his own piece no one marked the place with wax or made even the slightest indent with his finger-nail. They all took such care to acquaint themselves with what was to be recited that, when they were called upon to read unexpectedly, they performed so well that the Emperor never had occasion to reproach them. He indicated which of them he wished to read by pointing with his finger or his stick, or, if it was someone sitting far off, by sending a messenger from his entourage. He made it clear when he wanted the reading to stop by clearing his throat. Everyone listened very carefully for this sound. Whether it came at the end of a sentence, or in the middle of a clause, or even in a sub-clause, none of the subsequent readers dared to

begin farther back or farther on, however strange the beginning or end might seem. One result of this was that all those
in the place became excellent readers, even if they did not
understand what they read. No new arrival, not even if he
were famous, dared to join the Emperor's choir, unless he
could read and chant.

§8.   One day when Charlemagne was on a journey he came
to a great cathedral. A certain wandering monk, who was
unaware of the Emperor's attention to small detail, came into
the choir and, since he had never learned to do anything of the
sort himself, stood silent and confused in the middle of those
who were chanting. Thereupon the choir-master raised his
baton and threatened to hit him, if he did not sing. The monk,
not knowing what to do or where to turn, and not daring to
go out, twisted and contorted his throat, opened his mouth
wide, moved his bottom jaw up and down, and did all that
he could to imitate the appearance of someone singing. The
others present had not the self-control to stop laughing. Our
valiant Emperor, who was not to be moved from his serenity
by even the greatest events, sat solemnly waiting until the
end of the Mass, just as if he had not noticed this pretence at
singing. When it was all over, he called the poor wretch to
him and, taking pity on his struggles and the strain he had
gone through, consoled him with these words: 'My good
monk, thank you very much for your singing and your
efforts.' Then he ordered him to be given a pound of silver
to relieve his poverty.

§9.   I must not seem to forget or to neglect Alcuin.[9] I have
therefore recorded this true statement about his industry and
his accomplishments: of all his pupils there was not one who did
not distinguish himself by becoming a devout abbot or a famous
bishop. Grimald, my own master,[10] studied the liberal arts
under him, first in Gaul and then in Italy.[11] Lest I should be
accused by those who know the facts of telling a lie when I
say that there was no exception to this, there were, it is true,

among his pupils two sons of millers in the house of Saint
Columban who did not seem proper persons to be promoted
to the command of bishoprics or of monasteries; but through
the influence, as it is thought, of their master, these two acted
one after the other with great assiduity as stewards of the
monastery of Bobbio.

In this way the most glorious Charlemagne saw that the
study of letters was flourishing throughout the length and
breadth of his kingdom. All the same, despite his superhuman
efforts, he grieved because this scholarship was not reaching
the high standards of the early fathers, and in his dissatisfac-
tion he exclaimed: 'If only I could have a dozen churchmen
as wise and as well taught in all human knowledge as were
Jerome and Augustine!' The learned Alcuin, who considered
even himself ignorant in comparison with these two, became
very indignant at this, although he was careful not to show it,
and he dared to do what no one else would have done in the
presence of Charlemagne, for the Emperor struck terror into
everyone. 'The Maker of heaven and earth Himself,' he said,
'has very few scholars worth comparing with these men, and
yet you expect to find a dozen!'

§10.   At this point I must tell you a story which the people
of our time will find hard to accept. I myself, who am writing
it down, would scarcely believe it, were it not that I prefer to
rely upon the chance of our ancestors being truthful rather
than upon the lazy inaccuracy of men of our own period.
Charlemagne, who enjoyed divine service so much that he
never wearied of it, prided himself that he had achieved his
object of making all possible progress in the study of the
humanities. He was, however, greatly grieved by the fact
that all his provinces, and indeed his cities and even the smaller
localities, continued to differ in the way they worshipped
God, and particularly in the rhythm of their chanting. He
therefore asked Pope Stephen III of blessed memory, who,
according to the custom of his forefathers, had anointed

Charlemagne as ruler of the kingdom,[12] at the time when Childeric, that most cowardly King of the Franks, had been deposed and had his hair shorn, to send him some monks who were highly skilled in church singing.[13] The Pope, who was greatly pleased by the Emperor's pious request and by his enthusiasm, which was clearly divinely inspired, dispatched to him, in the land of the Franks, from his own apostolic see, a dozen monks well trained in chanting, the same number, that is, as there had been apostles. When I say the land of the Franks, I mean all the provinces north of the Alps; for, just as it is written: 'In those days it shall come to pass that ten men shall take hold out of all languages of the nations, even shall hold of the skirt of him that is a Jew',[14] so, at that time, because of the fame and glory of Charlemagne, the Gauls, the Aquitanians, the Aedui, the Spaniards, the Germans and the Bavarians all prided themselves on being paid a great compliment if they earned the right to be called Swabian Franks.

When the time came for these monks to set out from Rome, being, like all Greeks and Romans, greatly envious[15] of the glory of the Franks, they plotted among themselves to see how they could vary the ways of singing and so prevent the Franks in the kingdom and territory of Charlemagne from ever achieving uniformity. When they reported to Charlemagne they were received with honour, and they were apportioned out to a number of very famous places. Each in his own appointed locality began to chant with as much variation and as incorrectly as he knew how, and did all he could to teach others to do the same. Charlemagne, who was certainly no fool, celebrated the Feast of the Nativity and of the Coming of Christ at Trier or at Metz one year, and with great insight and attention to detail came to follow and understand the style of singing there; and the following year he took part in similar solemnities at Paris or at Tours, and there listened to singing which was completely different from what he had heard twelve months before at the other places mentioned. In the same way he discovered, as time went on, that the monks whom he had dispatched to the other cities were all different from each other in their singing. He reported this to Pope Leo of holy memory, who had succeeded to Stephen. Pope Leo recalled the monks to Rome and punished them with exile or life imprisonment. 'If I send you some more,' he said to the illustrious Charlemagne, 'they will be just as blind with envy as the first ones, and they will cheat you in their turn. This is how I will do what you wish. Send me two of the most intelligent monks whom you have in your own entourage, doing it in such a way that my own people do not find out that they belong to you. With God's help they will acquire the proficiency in this art which you are looking for.' Charlemagne did as Leo said. In a short time the two were perfectly trained and Leo sent them back to Charlemagne. One of them he kept with him. At the request of his own son, Drogo, Bishop of Metz, he sent the other one to the cathedral there.[16] Not only did this monk become most influential in Metz, but the effect of his teaching soon spread throughout all the land of the Franks, to such an extent that in our time church singing is called *Metz chant* by all those in those regions who use Latin. With us who speak the Teutonic or German language, it is called *Mette*; and in the Greek form the customary name is *Mettisca*. The holy Emperor had also ordered the second cantor, Peter by name, who had joined his own staff, to spend some short time at the monastery of Saint Gall. Here, too, he took care that church singing should be taught and learned according to the Roman fashion, and he presented to the monastery a standard antiphonary,[17] for he was an enthusiastic patron of Saint Gall. He gave the monastery many gifts of money and land, with houses[18] and rents[19] and other similar donations. He also presented the reliquary filled with relics and made of solid gold studded with gems, which is called the Shrine of Charles.

§11. Charlemagne, who was extremely temperate and God-fearing, had the habit of eating at the seventh hour in Lent, that is after Mass had been celebrated and after evening lauds. By so doing he was not breaking the fast, but was obeying the Lord's command by taking food an hour before the time. A certain bishop, who followed the letter of the law and had no common sense, and who thus ignored the wise man's maxim, was ill-advised enough to criticize the Emperor for doing this. Charlemagne in his wisdom concealed his anger, and received the bishop's criticism in all humility. 'My worthy bishop,' he answered, 'you have been within your rights to criticize me. In return, I order you to eat nothing yourself until the last of the officials who belong to my court here has been fed.'

When Charlemagne ate, he was waited on by dukes and chieftains and the kings of all sorts of peoples. These folk ate when he had finished, and they were served by counts and military commanders and nobles of various ranks. When these last came to the end of their meal, then army officers and the scholars of the court took their meal. After these came the heads of all the various ministries, then their officials, then the servants of these officials. In short, the last on the list received nothing to eat before midnight.

When Lent was nearly over and the bishop in question had endured his punishment day after day, Charlemagne, in his mercy, said to him: 'It seems to me, my dear bishop, that you must have realized by now that it is not greed which makes me eat before nightfall in Lent, but consideration for others.'

§12. On another occasion Charlemagne asked a bishop for his blessing. The bishop blessed the bread, ate some himself and then proposed to hand a piece to the noble Emperor. 'You can keep your bread for yourself,' said Charlemagne: and to the bishop's further mortification, he refused his blessing.

§13. Charlemagne was extremely prudent. He never gave

more than one piece of land at the same time to any of his counts, except to those who lived on the borders or confines of territory held by the barbarians. In the same way he never gave an abbey or any churches in the royal gift to a bishop, unless there were special reasons for doing so. When his advisers or his special friends asked him why he had this habit, he answered: 'With this revenue, or that estate, with no more than an abbey or a church, I can make as good a vassal out of some faithful retainer as any of my counts or bishops, and maybe even a better one!' When there were special reasons, he would give several rewards to the same people, as he did, for instance, to Uodalric, brother of the great Hildigard, the mother of kings and emperors. After the death of Hildigard, Charlemagne deprived Uodalric of his lands, because of something which he had done. A court jester said in the hearing of Charlemagne, who was a just ruler: 'Now that his sister is dead, Uodalric has lost his lands, those in the east and those in the west.' Charlemagne was moved to tears by these words; and he had all his former possessions restored to Uodalric.

As will be made clear in the second part of this work, when it seemed right to do so the Emperor gave munificent gifts to certain holy places.

§14. A particular bishopric lay directly in the Emperor's path whenever he set out on a journey, so that he could scarcely avoid visiting it. The bishop of the place was anxious to please Charlemagne and he put everything which he possessed at the Emperor's disposal. On one occasion Charlemagne arrived unexpectedly. The bishop was greatly upset. He flew hither and thither like a swallow and had not only his cathedral and the monks' dwellings but even the quadrangles and the courtyards cleaned and swept. Then he came forth to meet the Emperor, quite worn out and very indignant. Charlemagne, who was the most kindly of rulers, observed all this. He looked very carefully about him and inspected everything. Then he said to the bishop: 'My kind host, you always have everything carefully cleaned for my arrival!' The bishop, as if divinely inspired, bowed low, took the Emperor's unconquered right hand and kissed it, hid his irritation as best he could and answered: 'It is only right, my Lord, that, whenever you come, everything should be cleaned from top to bottom.' Charlemagne, the wisest of kings, quite understood what had happened. 'If I can empty,' he said, 'I can also fill.' Then he added: 'You may have the estate which is adjacent to your bishopric, you and all your successors, to the end of time.'

§15. Once, when making the same journey, Charlemagne visited without previous warning a certain bishop whose palace was on his direct route. It was the sixth day of the week, and on that day he was not prepared to eat the flesh of animals or birds. By the nature of the place the bishop was unable to provide fish except by previous arrangement. He ordered an excellent cheese, white with cream, to be served to the Emperor. Charlemagne, who was always moderate in his demands and ready for anything, no matter what the occasion, spared the blushes of the bishop and asked for nothing better. He picked up his knife, threw away the skin, which, so he thought, was not edible, and began to eat the white cheese. Then the bishop, who stood beside the Emperor to wait upon his wishes, took a step forward and asked: 'Why do you do that, my Lord Emperor? You are throwing away the best part.' The Emperor, who was incapable of deceiving others and did not expect others to deceive him, took the bishop's advice, put a piece of the skin in his mouth, chewed it slowly and swallowed it as if it were butter. The bishop had given him sensible advice. 'Good host,' he said, 'what you told me was true.' Then he added: 'Be sure to send to me every year in Aachen two cart-loads of cheeses just like this one.' The bishop was alarmed by the impossibility of the task, and, thinking that he was in danger of losing both his see and his rank, he answered: 'My Lord, I shall manage to find the cheeses; but I shall not be able to tell whether they are of this quality or not. I am afraid that I may lose favour with you as a result.' Nothing strange or unusual ever came amiss to Charlemagne. He said to the bishop, who had been familiar with cheeses all his life and yet seemed to know nothing about them: 'Cut them in two. Those which you see to be good join up again with a skewer, collect them in your cellar and then send them to me. Keep the rest for yourself, your clergy and your household.' This was done for two years, and the King ordered the gifts to be accepted without comment. The third year the bishop came himself and presented in person the cheeses which he had collected with such difficulty over a long period. Then Charlemagne, who was a just man, took pity on his bishop's trials and tribulations. He presented a rich estate to the bishopric, from which the bishop and his successors could draw as much corn and wine as they and their dependants could possibly need.

§16. We have shown how, in his wisdom, Charlemagne exalted the humble. Let us now tell how he humbled the proud. There was a certain bishop who was vainglorious and greatly preoccupied with all manner of stupid things. Charlemagne was highly observant, and he came to hear of this. He gave instructions to a Jewish merchant, who often visited the Holy Land and was in the habit of bringing home across the sea many rare and wonderful objects, that he was to cheat and deceive this bishop in any way he cared.

The Jew caught an ordinary house mouse. He stuffed it with various spices and then offered it for sale to the bishop, pretending that he had brought home from Judea a most costly creature never before seen by man. The bishop was overjoyed at such an opportunity and offered the Jew three pounds of silver in exchange for so remarkable a piece of merchandise. 'A fine price for such an unusual object!' exclaimed the Jew. 'I would rather throw it into the sea than let anyone acquire it at so cheap and shameful a price!' The bishop was rich, for he never gave anything to the poor and needy. He promised the Jew ten pounds, if he could have this incomparable oddity. The clever merchant pretended to lose his temper and replied: 'May the God of Abraham forbid that I should lose my labour in this way, and the cost of the transport, too!' The greedy bishop, his mouth agape with desire for the costly rarity, offered him twenty pounds. The Jew became angrier still. He wrapped the mouse in precious silk and prepared to leave. Then the bishop, deceived and indeed thoroughly open to deception, called him back and offered him a full measure of silver, if only he could have the priceless object. At long last the merchant yielded to his entreaties and gave in, although with much show of reluctance. He took the money which he had received to the Emperor and told him all that had happened.

A few days later the King called all the bishops and the chief men of that province to a council. Inevitably there was much preliminary discussion, after which he ordered all the silver to be produced and placed in the middle of his palace. He then spoke himself. 'Elders, stewards, bishops of our Church,' said he, 'it is your duty to minister to the poor, or rather to Jesus Christ in the persons of the poor, and not to waste your substance on stupid objects. Nowadays you act completely to the contrary; and, even more than other mortals, you are guilty of luxury and covetousness.' Then he added: 'One of your number has given all this silver to a Jew in exchange for a painted mouse.' The bishop who had been so cruelly deceived, ran forward and threw himself at the Emperor's feet, begging forgiveness for his sin. Charlemagne upbraided him as he deserved and then let him take himself off in confusion.

§17. The same bishop was left in charge of the renowned Hildigard, when the great warrior Charlemagne was engaged in battle against the Huns.[20] He was so over-excited by his close relationship with the Queen, and he became so impudent as a result, that he dared to ask if he could borrow the golden sceptre of the peerless Charlemagne, which the Emperor had ordered to be made for his own ceremonial use, so that it could be carried as a wand of honour on festal days in place of his episcopal staff. Hildigard dealt with him cleverly enough, for she said that she dare not entrust the sceptre to anyone, but that she would without fail see that the request was put to the King. When Charlemagne returned home, Hildigard laughingly told him what the mad bishop had asked. The Emperor, too, was greatly amused and he agreed to do what Hildigard had asked, saying that he would go even further than she had suggested. When almost everyone of any importance from the whole of Europe had gathered together to congratulate Charlemagne on his triumph over so powerful a people, he made this speech in the hearing of all, both great and small: 'Bishops should be contemptuous of this world and by their example inspire others to turn to heavenly matters. Nowadays, however, they are even more puffed up with ambition than other mortals. One of them, not content with his rank of bishop, which he holds in the most important episcopal see in Germany,[21] has dared, without our even having been consulted, to claim our own golden sceptre, which we bear as an emblem of our royal might, so that he could use it as a pastoral staff.'

The guilty man, who acknowledged his sin, was pardoned by the Emperor, and left hurriedly.

§18. I am very much afraid that if I carry out your command, my Lord and Emperor Charles,[22] I shall incur the enmity of all those in holy orders and more especially that of the higher clergy. However, as long as I am assured of your protection, I do not propose to worry very much about these people.

It happened on one occasion that the pious Emperor Charlemagne decreed that all the bishops throughout the length and breadth of his empire should, before a certain day which he himself had chosen, deliver a sermon in the cathedral church of their diocese. Anyone who failed to do so was to be dismissed from the honour of being a bishop. (Why do I say from the honour? The apostle declares: 'If a man desire the office of a bishop, he desireth a good work.'[23] The truth is, as I am prepared to admit to you in private, most serene of kings, that there is great honour to be had in this position, but there is not the slightest need for good work.) The bishop about whom I have been telling you was at first greatly frightened by this order, for fine living and arrogant behaviour were really the sum total of his knowledge, and if he were to be dismissed from his bishopric he would at the same time be cut off from his luxurious way of life.

One feast day he invited two of the nobles of the court to his cathedral. After the reading of the lesson, he mounted the pulpit as if he were going to address the congregation. The people all gathered together in amazement at so unexpected a happening, except one poor red-headed fellow, who stood balancing one of his boots on top of his head, for he had no cap and he was very self-conscious about the colour of his hair. The bishop, who held his rank in name rather than in deed, said to his sexton (he was more of a beadle [24] than a door-keeper and, indeed, men of his rank and function were called aediles by the ancient Romans): 'Bring me that man with his head covered, the one standing near the door of the church.' The sexton hurried off to obey his lord's command. He seized hold of the unfortunate man and began to drag him towards the bishop. The man struggled with all his might and main to avoid being brought before the judgement seat of so stern a magistrate, for he was afraid of being punished with great severity for daring to stand in the house of God with his head covered. The bishop glared down from his lofty position. In a mighty voice he began his sermon, which seemed to be at one and the same time an exhortation to his flock and a general condemnation of his miserable victim. 'Drag him here! Mind he doesn't escape! You must come here, my man, whether you want to or not.' By main force and in sheer panic the man was compelled to come near. 'Come nearer still!' intoned the bishop. 'You must come quite close to me!' He then snatched off his victim's head-covering and announced to the congregation: 'Lo and behold, all you people! This fool is red-headed!' He then turned to the altar and went through the ceremony of Mass, or at least gave a fair imitation of doing so.

When Mass was over, they walked across to the bishop's palace, which was adorned with carpets of every colour and tapestries of every kind. The banquet which followed was served so lavishly, on gold plate and silver, and in vessels studded with jewels, that it was capable of tickling the palate of even the most dainty eaters, or of those so gross with food already that the sight of more might have given them nausea. The bishop sat on the softest of cushions. He was dressed in the most precious of silken stuffs and wore the imperial purple. Indeed, he was a king, in all but name and sceptre. He was surrounded by troops of military attendants who were so richly accoutred that in comparison with them the two men from the court, noblemen of the unconquered Charlemagne, were ashamed of their own mean appearance. At the end of this magnificent banquet, the equal of which it would be hard to find even in royal circles, they stepped forward to take their leave. Thereupon, in order to demonstrate to them even more clearly his own magnificence and glory, the bishop ordered skilled choristers to advance: they were accompanied by every musical instrument one could think of, and by the sound of their singing they could have softened the hardest hearts or turned to ice the limpid waters of the Rhine. Every imaginable variety of drink, mixed with all kinds of flavouring and colouring-matter, garlanded with herbs and flowers, which set off the gleam of the jewels and the gold and at the same time imparted a new sheen to them, grew luke-warm in their hands, for their stomachs could take no more. At the same time pastry-cooks, roasters of meat, bakers of fine bread and stuffers of chicken were striving to stimulate their appetite with the viands which they had prepared with such artistry; but, alas, their bellies were full. Such a banquet had never been offered to the great Charlemagne himself.

Morning came. The bishop returned to sobriety, more or less. He shuddered to think of the extravagance which he had paraded so openly before the King's representatives. He ordered them to be summoned back to his presence. He loaded them with presents worthy of royalty, and he implored them to be so kind as to tell the mighty Charlemagne of the goodness and simplicity of his way of life, stressing particularly that he had preached a public sermon in his own cathedral, with them in the congregation.

When they arrived home, the Emperor asked why the bishop had invited them. They fell at his feet and answered: 'Master, it was so that he could honour us, in your name, far beyond our own humble deserts.' They went on: 'This particular bishop is most faithful to you, he is the best of them all and worthy of the highest rank in the Church. If you are willing to trust our poor judgement, we proclaim to your sublime majesty that we heard him preach with great eloquence.' The Emperor was not unaware of the bishop's ineptitude. He questioned them about his style of preaching; and they described it in detail, for they did not dare to deceive him. The Emperor realized that it was through fear of him that the bishop had tried to make some pronouncement in public, rather than dare to disobey his order. He accordingly permitted him to retain his rank of bishop, however unworthy he knew him to be of it.

§19.   Some time after this a young man who was a relation of the King's sang the Alleluia most beautifully at some feast day or other. The Emperor turned to this same bishop and said: 'That young man of ours sang well!' The bishop was so stupid that he took this to be a joke, and in any case he did not know that the young man was a relation of the Emperor. 'Country bumpkins drone on just like that,' said he, 'when they are following their oxen at the plough.' At this outrageous answer the Emperor glared fiercely at the bishop and struck the astonished man to the ground.

§20.   There was another bishop of a minute township who, while he still lived in the flesh, wanted to be worshipped with divine honour, instead of being considered merely as one who interceded with God, as were the apostles and martyrs. However, he was determined to conceal his arrogance, so that he could continue to be called a holy man of God, and not be execrated along with all the other idols worshipped by the people. Among his townsfolk he had a certain retainer, not of low birth, but a man quick to act and full of energy. I will not say that this man did the bishop any particular favour, and he certainly did not fawn upon him when he spoke. In fact he was not quite sure what he could do to please his bishop, who was a harsh man. He decided that he might find favour in the bishop's eyes if he could prove that he had performed some miracle in his name. Whenever he set out from his home to visit the bishop, he led on a leash two little bitches, of the breed called *veltres*[25] in French. In view of their speed these dogs could easily catch foxes and other small animals, and what is more they would often seize quails[26] and other birds which flush quickly. One day, as he rode along, the man saw a fox sitting on one of the stone walls. Without a word he suddenly set his dogs after it. They rushed after the fox at full speed and came up with it in a single bow-shot. The man followed behind as fast as he could and wrested the fox alive and unharmed from the teeth and claws of the dogs. He tied the dogs in a suitable spot and hurried joyfully off to his master with his gift. He went in to the bishop and said to him humbly: 'My Lord, just see what sort of a gift I have been able to find for you.' The bishop laughed and asked him how he had been able to capture the fox without harming it. The man went closer to him, swore by his master's good health that he would not conceal the truth and then answered: 'My Lord, I was riding through the field back there. I saw this fox, which was quite close to me. Letting my reins fall loose, I began to ride after it. Then, when the fox was so far away that I could scarcely see it any more, I raised my hand and addressed it in these words: "In the name of my master Recho,[27] be still and go no step farther." Lo and behold, the fox stood fast on that spot, as if it had been chained to the ground, until I picked it up, just as if it were a lost sheep.' The bishop swelled up with empty pride and said in the hearing of all: 'Now my divinity is quite clear. Now I know who I am and now I recognize what I shall be.' From that day onwards he showed greater affection to this execrable man than to anyone else in his household.

§21. Since the occasion has offered itself, although indeed they have nothing to do with my subject matter, it does not seem to be a bad idea to add these two stories to my official narrative, together with a few more which happened at the same time and are worthy of being recorded.

In New Frankland there lived a certain bishop who was of remarkable saintliness and abstinence and at the same time unique in his liberality and his compassion. The Devil, who hates any form of righteousness, was greatly exasperated by this bishop's virtue: he aroused in him so great a desire of eating meat in Lent that the bishop thought he would die of debility and languor unless he could be restored to strength by some meat dish. The bishop was reassured by a great many holy men, venerable fathers and priests, who advised him that he must eat flesh in order to regain his health. Driven on by ultimate necessity, he yielded to their authority, for, if he had not obeyed them, he might have been held to have destroyed his own life. In the end he placed in his mouth a morsel of flesh from a four-footed animal.

The moment the bishop began to chew the meat and to savour its taste hesitantly on his palate, he was immediately seized by a dislike, nay, by a loathing, not only for meat but for all other foodstuffs, for the very light of day and for life here below itself, and by a consequent despair for his own life. The result was that he would no longer eat or drink, and he placed his sole hope in the Saviour of sinners. As the first week of Lent passed by, the above-mentioned fathers suggested to him that, as he was fully aware that he was being deceived by an hallucination sent by the Devil, he should make every effort to vanquish his one momentary peccadillo, to make amends for it and to wash it away, by means of even harsher fasts, by heartfelt grief and by lavish alms. He again yielded to their advice, as all in their wisdom advised him to do. In an attempt to confound the malice of the Devil and to obtain pardon for his sin from Him who restores innocence, he inflicted on himself two-day fasts and even three-day fasts, he abandoned altogether the quiet peace of sleep, and he ministered every day with his own hands to the poor and to pilgrims, washing their feet, giving them clothes and money to the full extent of his means, and wishing even to go beyond his means. On the holy day of Easter Saturday, he collected large wine-jars from the entire city and ordered that hot baths be prepared for all the poor from dawn to dusk. With his own hand he shaved the throats of all those who wished it, and with his nails he removed purulent scabs and hairy growths from their hirsute bodies. He then anointed them with unguents and dressed them in white garments, as a sign of their regeneration.

When at length the sun moved round to the west and there remained no one who had not submitted to these attentions, the bishop himself stepped into a bath. When he emerged, his conscience was clear, and he dressed himself in spotless raiment, so that, with the approval of all holy churchmen, he might celebrate Mass with the people. Just as he approached his church, the cunning Devil, who wanted to nullify what the bishop had determined to do, by making it seem that he had failed in his vow and had left at least one poor man uncleansed, assumed the appearance of a filthy and really ghastly leper, with running pus and the rags of his clothing stiff with putrefaction, and so came to meet him on the threshold of the building, with tottering and palsied step, and the hoarse voice of one in utter misery. The saintly bishop was inspired from above to turn towards him and to recognize the Devil, to whom he had so recently succumbed. He stripped off his white clothes, ordered more water to be heated immediately and had the leper placed in it. Then he seized hold of a razor and began to shave away at the Devil's filthy throat. As soon as he shaved all the hair off his windpipe from one ear to the middle, he began again at the other ear and so scraped away until he came back to the same spot. The remarkable thing was that when he reached the middle with his razor a second time he found that the long bristles which he had previously cut away had grown again. This happened several times without the bishop pausing in his labours with the razor. Then lo and behold an eye of such extraordinary size that I shudder when I describe it began to appear in the centre of the Devil's windpipe, between the very hands of the bishop-turned-barber. The bishop, who was terrified at the sight of such a monstrosity, sprang to his feet and with a great shout crossed himself in the name of Christ. A second before this invocation the cunning Devil, who was unable to hide his stratagem any longer, disappeared into smoke. As he went he said: 'This eye was watching you carefully when you ate meat on a fast-day.'

§22.   In the same neighbourhood there lived another bishop who was of incomparable saintliness. With improvident composure, as one still hardly aware of the female sex, he permitted young nuns to converse with him as pupils, in addition to the priests of mature years. During the feast of Easter, at the conclusion of the divine service which lasted until well after midnight, he indulged himself rather too freely with an Alsatian wine from Sigoltesheim,[28] as well as with some Falernian, which is even stronger. In his ensuing state of bewilderment, he conjured up in his mind the form and the meretricious gestures of a most beautiful woman and, when the others had retired to rest, he dreamt that he called her to his bed and in a miserable moment had intercourse with her. At the first red glow of dawn, he rose quickly and in the company of his household washed away in running water the memory of the night. Then, with his conscience far from clear, he moved forward before the all-seeing eyes of the true Godhead. When the first music was over and the moment came for him to begin the angelic hymn, according to his duty, he was struck with fear and remained silent. He placed on top of the altar the vestments which he was wearing for his holy office, turned to the congregation and confessed his sin. Then he ran to the foot of the altar and dissolved into a vast flood of tears. The congregation insisted that he should get up, and with awful oaths demanded that on that day especially the ceremony of the Mass should not be celebrated for them by anyone else but their own bishop. The bishop could not be moved and this controversy continued for a period of nearly three hours. In the end Almighty God in his clemency took pity on the vows of the devoted congregation and the contrite heart of the bishop. He was dressed again in his vestments as he lay on the floor and, once more assured of God's indulgence, was mercifully raised up to perform the holy and awe-inspiring mysteries, either as an example of true penitence, or as a warning that safety is nowhere and never sure in this earthly existence, for it is always and everywhere illusory.

§23. In what is known as Old Frankland there lived another bishop who was uncommonly parsimonious. When, in a certain abnormal year, the failure of all the crops in this district laid waste the entire neighbourhood, this miserly landlord, rejoicing in the ultimate necessity of all the inhabitants, who were already on the point of death, ordered his storehouses to be opened, so that supplies could be offered for sale at an exorbitant price.

A certain devil of the type called hobgoblins, whose particular function it is to foster the petty foibles and deceits of human beings, had the habit of visiting the dwelling of a local blacksmith and of passing the night by playing with the man's hammers and anvils. When this father of a family tried to protect himself and his possessions with the sign of the all-healing Cross, the shaggy devil replied: 'My dear fellow, if you will agree not to stop me amusing myself in your smithy, put your drinking-pot[29] here and each day you will find it full.' The poor blacksmith was more afraid of dying of hunger and thirst than he was of the eternal damnation of his soul, and he did what the devil asked of him. The devil took a huge flask, broke repeatedly into the cellar of the blacksmith's Bacchus or Dis, to wit the bishop, stole what he wanted and left the remainder running all over the floor. A great many barrels were emptied in this way and the bishop finally came to the conclusion that they had been wasted by some gigantic fraud perpetrated by devils. He sprinkled his store-room with holy water and protected it with the sign of the invincible Cross. When night fell once more, the hobgoblin came back with his flask. He did not dare to touch the wine-barrels because of the holy Cross, and he could not find his way out again. He was discovered there in human form and bound by the watchman of the house. He was led before the people as a thief and executed publicly. As he was being dispatched, he exclaimed: 'Woe is me, I have lost my dear friend's drinking-pot!'

I have set this story down, because it ought to be known, provided always that this tale is a true one, that things denied on oath may yet turn out well, and so may things hidden, in the days of necessity; and that, whatever be the worth of the invocation of the Holy Name, it can be used, too, by those who do evil.

§24.   While I have been devoting my attention to the chief state of the Franks, and also examining its dependencies, I have lost sight of some of the most important and, indeed, also some of the less notable of the other races. I must now turn to our near neighbours, the Italians, who are divided from us by a single wall of mountains.

There lived in that country a bishop who was a great collector of useless objects. The Devil observed this fact. He appeared in human form before a certain poor man who was of miserly habits. The Devil promised this poor man that he would become extremely rich if only he would bind himself to him for ever with the articles of partnership. The miser was quite ready to take advantage of this offer. The cunning Devil then made this proposition to him: 'I am going to convert myself into a very fine mule. Climb on my back and ride to the bishop's courtyard. When he begins to show eagerness to buy the mule, drag the matter out, put off your decision, say that you cannot agree to the sale, put up your price, pretend that you are offended, and even prepare to leave. Then it must follow that he will press you hard and make you many promises. In the end be prevailed upon by his entreaties and, when you have received in exchange a great amount of money, sell him the mule, pretending that it is against your will and your better judgement. Then make your retreat as quickly as you can and go off somewhere to hide.'

All this was done. The bishop, who was unable to wait until the following day, mounted his steed that very noon, in the full flush of excitement, with the intention of parading proudly through his city. The mule dashed off at full speed into the open country and hastened to a river to cool itself in the water. In this way a long period passed, as the mule enjoyed itself to the full, advancing with a zigzag motion, running at full speed and dashing hither and thither like a school of dolphins. In the end the ancient Belial, impatient of spur and rein, and sweating as with the fires of Hell, began to hurl himself into the depths of a whirlpool and to drag the bishop in with him. With great difficulty the bishop was pulled out by the zeal and firm hand of a group of fishermen, who happened to be sailing by.

§25. The Devil, who is skilful in laying ambushes and is in the habit of setting snares for us in the road which we are to follow, is not slow to trip us up one after another by means of some vice or other. The crime of fornication was imputed to a certain princely bishop – in such a case the name must be omitted. This matter came to the notice of his congregation, and then through tale-tellers it eventually reached the ears of the most pious Charles, the chief bishop of them all. He in his wisdom let the matter lie for some time, for he was unwilling to give credence to idle stories, but

> Rumour, the swiftest traveller of all the ills on earth,
> Thriving on movement,[30]

exceeds the size of eagles, from being as small as a tomtit,[31] so that it strives in vain to be concealed. Charlemagne, that most rigorous searcher after justice, sent two of his court officials who were to turn aside that evening to a place near to the city in question and then come unexpectedly to the bishop at first light and ask him to celebrate Mass for them. If he should refuse, then they were to compel him in the name of the Emperor to celebrate the Holy Mysteries in person. The bishop did not know what to do, for that very night he had sinned before the eyes of the Heavenly Observer, and yet he did not dare to offend his visitors. Fearing men more than he feared God, he bathed his sweaty limbs in ice-cold spring-water and then went forward to offer the awe-inspiring sacraments. Behold, either his conscience gripped his heart tight, or the water penetrated his veins, for he was seized with such frosty chill that no attention from his doctors was of use to him. He was brought to his death by a frightful attack of fever and compelled to submit his soul to the decree of the strict and eternal Judge.

§26.   However much the rest of mankind may be deceived by these wiles of the Devil and his attendant demons, and by others of the same nature, we gain comfort by meditating on the word of our Lord, who, when he came to reward the unequivocal confession of Saint Peter, said to him: 'Thou art Peter, and upon this rock I will build my church; and the gates of hell shall not prevail against it.'[32] In fulfilment of this promise, He has ordained that His church should remain inviolate and unmoved, even in these days of great danger and wickedness.

It is true that jealousy is always rife between rivals: and that is why it has been a constant habit of the inhabitants of Rome to oppose and to be the constant enemies of every Pope of any influence who over the centuries has been raised to the Apostolic See. It happened as a result that certain Romans who were blind with envy accused the above-mentioned Pope Leo of blessed memory of a mortal crime, and then tried to put his eyes out. By God's will they lost heart and drew back at the last moment. They were unsuccessful in their attempt to gouge out the Pope's eyes, but they slashed him across the face with their knives.[33]

Through his servants Pope Leo sent news of this in secret to Michael, the Emperor of Constantinople.[34] Michael refused to help him. 'The Pope has his own royal power,' said he, 'and it is greater than ours. He himself must take vengeance on his enemies.'

Thereupon his Holiness invited the unconquered Charlemagne to come to Rome. In this he followed God's will: for, since Charlemagne was already ruler and emperor of so many people in his own right, he should now in his glory be granted

the title of Emperor and Caesar Augustus by the authority of
the Apostolic See.[35] Charlemagne was always ready at a
moment's notice to set out in full martial array. Although he
was completely ignorant of the reason for the summons,[36]
he, the head of the world, set out immediately for the city
which had hitherto held that position. When the wicked
people of Rome learned of his unexpected coming, they took
flight and concealed themselves in various hideouts, cellars
and lurking-places, just as little birds hide when they hear the
voice of their master. Nowhere under heaven could they
escape from his energetic and shrewd search: and they were
captured and brought in chains to the cathedral of Saint
Peter. There Leo, this incorrupt Pope, took the gospel of our
Lord Jesus Christ, held it above his head, and in the hearing
not only of Charlemagne and his soldiers but also of those who
had persecuted him, swore the following oath: 'As I hope on
the great Judgement Day to have my share in this gospel, I
am guiltless of the crime of which these men have falsely
accused me.'[37] Many of the prisoners begged that they might
be allowed to swear on the tomb of Saint Peter that they too
were guiltless of the crime imputed to them. The Pope was
quite aware of their dishonesty. 'I beg you, unconquered
servant of God,' said he to Charlemagne, 'not to be deceived
by their cunning. They know very well that Saint Peter is
always willing to forgive. Look among the tombs of the
martyrs for the stone on which is written the name of the
thirteen-year-old boy Saint Pancras. If they swear to you by his
name, then you may be sure of them.' What the Pope had
ordered was done.[38] A crowd of people came forward to take
their oath on this stone, but some of them fell down dead and
the others were seized by the Devil and went mad. Then
Charlemagne in his mighty power said to his men: 'Do not
let one of them escape.'[39] They were all seized and condemned
to a variety of deaths, or else imprisoned for life.

Charlemagne stayed a few days more in Rome, in order to

rest his army. The Bishop of the Apostolic See called together such people as he could from the neighbouring districts and then, in their presence and that of all the unconquered comrades-in-arms of the glorious Charlemagne, who, himself, of course, expected nothing of the kind, Leo pronounced him Emperor and Defender of the Church of Rome. Charlemagne could not refuse what was offered, the more so as he believed that it was pre-ordained by God, but he did not receive his new titles with any great pleasure.[40] His immediate reaction was that the Greeks would be filled with even greater jealousy than before and that they would plan some disaster for the Frankish kingdom. If nothing more, they would prepare themselves still more carefully against the day when Charlemagne should arrive unexpectedly to subdue their kingdom and add it to his own empire, as he was rumoured to be about to do. Above all, the mighty Charlemagne remembered how the legates of the King of Constantinople had come and had told him that their master wished to be his faithful friend; and that, seeing that they were destined to become nearer neighbours, he was determined to support Charlemagne as if he were his own son, and to relieve his poverty; and how, unable to hide his passionate ambition in his heart, he himself had shouted: 'If only that narrow strait of water did not separate us! Perhaps we could divide between us the riches of the East, or else hold them in common and each have his own fair share!' This is the sort of thing which those who know nothing of African poverty have a habit of saying about the kings of the Africans![41]

The Lord God, who is at once the giver and restorer of health, gave proof of the innocence of the blessed Leo. He restored his eyesight, making it stronger than it had been before this wicked and inhuman blow with a knife. As a sign of Leo's innocence, a shining scar, as white as driven snow, ran across his dove-like eyes, in the shape of a very thin line.[42]

§27. I must not be accused of ignorance by those who know no better because I reported that the sea, which our great Emperor called a narrow strait of water, was said by him to lie between us and the Greeks. Indeed, as all who want to know are already aware, at that time the Huns, the Bulgarians and many other savage races barred the overland route to Greece, with their armies intact and unbroken. Later on the most warlike Charlemagne conquered some of these peoples, the Slavs, for example, and the Bulgarians. He destroyed the entire population and the very name of the Huns, those men of iron and adamant. I will go into these matters later on, after I have given a very short account of the buildings which Charlemagne, Emperor and Caesar Augustus, following the example of Solomon in his great wisdom, caused to be constructed on a magnificent scale at Aachen, some of them in God's honour, others for himself and the remainder for all the bishops, abbots, counts and other guests who flocked there from all over the world.

§28. Whenever Charlemagne, who was the most energetic of Emperors, had the opportunity of resting a while, he preferred to labour in the service of God rather than relax at his ease. He conceived the idea of constructing on his native soil and according to his own plan a cathedral which should be finer than the ancient buildings of the Romans.[43] Soon he was able to congratulate himself on having accomplished his wish. To help him in this building he summoned from all the lands beyond the seas architects and workmen skilled in every relevant art. He placed in charge of them all a certain abbot who was most experienced in this sort of work, but of whose fraudulent habits Charlemagne was completely unaware. As soon as the Emperor's back was turned, this man began to accept bribes and to let any man return home who wished to do so. Those who were unable to buy themselves out, or whom their masters refused to release, he burdened with immense tasks, just as the Egyptians once exacted inhuman labour from God's own people. He collected a vast store of gold, silver and silken cloth by this fraudulent behaviour. In his room he displayed only the least precious articles, and the more valuable things he hid in boxes and chests. One day people suddenly reported to him that his house was on fire. He came running over and forced his way through the mass of flames[44] into the room where the chests of gold were kept. He was not satisfied to rescue one box: he loaded a treasure-chest on to the shoulders of each of his servants, and only then turned to make his escape. As he emerged, a huge beam which had been dislodged by the fire fell on top of him. His body was consumed by earthly flames at the very moment when his soul was journeying off to the everlasting bonfire. In this way the Judgement of God kept watch for the devout Emperor Charlemagne, when his own attention was turned elsewhere by the affairs of his kingdom.

§29.   There was another craftsman whose skill at moulding bronze and glass was greater than that of anyone else in the world. His name was Tancho and he had formerly been a monk at Saint Gall. He cast a superb bell, and the Emperor was delighted with its tone. This outstanding worker in bronze, who was doomed all the same to a terrible fate, said to the Emperor: 'My Imperial master, order a great mass of copper to be delivered to me and I will refine it. Then, instead of tin, give me as much silver as I need, a hundred pounds at least. I will cast you such a bell that this one will seem dumb in comparison.' Charlemagne, who was the most open-handed of monarchs – if riches abounded, he set not his heart upon them[45] – made no difficulty about ordering everything for which he had asked to be given to him. The rascally monk took delivery of the materials and left in great glee. He smelted and refined the bronze. Instead of the silver he used the purest tin and soon cast a bell much better than that made of adulterated metal, of which Charlemagne had nevertheless thought so highly. When he had tested the new bell, he presented it to the Emperor. Charlemagne admired the new bell very much for its exquisite shape. He ordered an iron clapper to be fixed inside and then had the bell hung in the bell-tower. This was soon done. The churchwarden, the other attendants in the church and even a number of boys who were hanging about all strove, one after the other, to make the bell ring. None of them succeeded. In the end the monk who had cast the bell and perpetrated this outrageous fraud came over in a rage, seized hold of the rope and tugged at the bell. The mass of metal slipped from the centre of its beam and fell down on the rogue's head. It passed straight through his dead carcase and crashed to the ground, taking his bowels and testicles with it. When the mass of silver of which I have told you was discovered, Charlemagne in his justice ordered it to be distributed among the poor of his palace.

§30. It was a rule in those days that whenever the Emperor had ordered some building project to be carried out – the construction of bridges, ships or causeways, or the cleansing, paving or levelling of muddy roads – the counts of the Empire could operate through deputies and lesser officials, always provided that only minor works were concerned. From major works, and especially new constructions, no duke, count, bishop or abbot could be excused, whatever the pretext. The arches of the great bridge at Mainz can be quoted as examples of this rule. All Europe, so to speak, laboured side by side at this bridge in orderly cooperation; and then the fraudulent behaviour of a few malevolent people, who were determined to amass some ill-gotten gain from the ships passing underneath, brought about its destruction.[46]

If there were any churches belonging to the royal domain which needed to be decorated with carved ceilings or wall-paintings, this was attended to by the bishops and abbots of the neighbourhood. If, on the other hand, new churches had to be built, all bishops, dukes, counts, abbots, those in charge of churches in the King's gift and anyone who held a public office worked at them ceaselessly from the foundations to the roof. This is proved not only by the cathedral at Aachen, which was built by human hands, yet with the inspiration of God. It is also proved by the mansions belonging to men of various rank which were erected round the palace of Charlemagne in such a way that, shrewd as he was, through the windows of his private apartment, he could see everything they were doing, and all their comings and goings, without their realizing it. In the same way all the houses of his nobles were built high off the ground, so that the retainers of his nobles, the personal servants of those retainers and every other passer-by could be protected from rain or snow, cold or heat, and yet the nobles themselves could not hide from the eyes of the ever-vigilant Charlemagne. The description of this cathedral I leave to your own court officials, for I myself am tied here in my monastery. I return, instead, to an account of the Judgement of God, which was made manifest in its precincts.

§31. Charlemagne, who was a provident ruler, ordered certain nobles who lived in the neighbourhood to give every possible assistance to the workmen whom he had engaged, and to do all in their power to supply the materials necessary for building the cathedral. The workmen had come from far away. He put them in the care of a man called Liutfrid,[47] who was steward of the palace, telling him to feed and clothe them at public expense and to be very careful to provide immediately anything which proved necessary for the building. As long as Charlemagne remained in residence Liutfrid did this with considerable zeal. The moment the Emperor left, his steward stopped altogether, and amassed so much money by maltreating the miserable workmen that Dis and Pluto would require the help of a camel to carry all his ill-gotten gains away to Hell.

This was revealed to mortal men in the following way. Our glorious Emperor Charlemagne had the habit of going to lauds at night in a long flowing cloak, the use and the very name of which are now forgotten. When the early-morning hymns were over, he would return to his room and dress himself in his imperial robes ready for the morning functions. All the churchmen used to come ready robed to these services, which took place just before dawn, either in the church itself or in an ante-room which was then called the outer court. There they would stand awaiting the moment when the Emperor should step forward to attend the celebration of Mass, and if anyone was overcome with sleep he would rest his head awhile on his companion's chest. Once, as a certain miserable clerk among their number, who used – so poor were the amenities of the palace – to go to the house of this man Liutfrid to have his clothes, or perhaps I should say his rags, washed and mended, lay sleeping with his head on the knees of a friend, he saw in a vision a giant, taller than the adversary of Saint Anthony, emerge from the King's court and hurry across the streamlet over a bridge towards the steward's house. Behind him he led an enormous camel, on which was loaded an incredible amount of wealth. The clerk was filled with amazement at what he saw in his dream. He asked the giant where he had come from and where he wanted to go. The giant answered: 'I come from the King's house and I am going to the house of Liutfrid. I propose to perch Liutfrid on top of all these bundles and to lead him off to Hell with them.'

The clerk, who was terrified in his mind lest Charlemagne, whom he greatly feared, should discover that he was asleep, was in effect awakened by this dream. He looked up, made sure that the others were awake and then began to address them. 'Will you please listen to what I have just dreamed?' he asked. 'I seemed to see Polyphemus himself,[48] who reached to the stars as he walked on the earth, and who passed through the Ionian Sea without wetting his mighty flanks. I saw him hurry from the King's court into Liutfrid's house, with a heavily laden camel. When I asked the reason why he was doing this, he replied: "I am going to perch Liutfrid on top of this luggage and lead him off to Hell." '

He had not yet reached the end of his story when a girl came out of the steward's house, a girl whom they all knew. She fell at their feet and begged them to remember her friend Liutfrid in their prayers. They asked her why she said this. 'My lords,' she answered, 'he went out to the lavatory in good health. He was there longer than was necessary, and when we came to look for him we found that he was dead.'

The sudden death of Liutfrid was announced to the Emperor. His grasping avarice was described at some length by his workmen and servants, and Charlemagne ordered that his possessions should be examined. They were found to be of priceless worth. When the greatest judge beneath God learned just how they had been acquired, he announced this decision to those present: 'None of these possessions which he gained so fraudulently can go towards saving his miserable soul. They must be divided between the workmen engaged on this building of ours and the poor of our palace.'

§32.   There are two other tales to be told of events which occurred in the same place. There was a certain deacon who followed the habits of the Italians in that he was perpetually trying to resist nature. He used to take baths, he had his head very closely shaved, he polished his skin, he cleaned his nails, he had his hair cut as short as if it had been turned on a lathe, and he wore linen underclothes and a snow-white shirt. Then, because he did not wish to miss his turn, or maybe because he thought he would appear even more splendid doing this, he proceeded of his own free will to read the Holy Gospel in the presence of Almighty God and His holy angels, and in the sight of our austere King and his nobles. Just how unclean his heart was became apparent by what followed. As he was reading, a spider suddenly came down on its thread from the ceiling, touched the deacon's head with its feeler and then ran quickly up again. Charlemagne, keenly observant, saw this happen a second and third time, but he pretended not to notice it. Since the Emperor was looking at him, the clerk did not dare to protect himself with his hand, especially as he thought that he was being attacked by flies rather than by a spider. He finished his reading of the Gospel and went through the remainder of the service. When he came out of the cathedral, he began to swell up. Within an hour he was dead. Charlemagne, the most devout of kings, considered himself guilty of the man's death, because he had observed the cause of the danger and had done nothing to prevent it. He therefore insisted on doing public penance.

§33. The glorious Charlemagne had among his retinue a certain clerk who was a veritable paragon. It was said of him what has never been said of any other human being, that he excelled all other men in his knowledge of secular and divine literature, in the singing of both church and popular music, in the composition of poems and in their recitation, and above all in the sweet fullness of his voice and the inestimable pleasure which he gave when he spoke.

Moses, the law-giver, who was filled with wisdom by the teaching of God, made a pretext of the thinness of his voice[49] and of the sluggishness of his tongue, and therefore sent someone else in his place, a man who, by the authority of God who dwelt within him, controlled even the heavenly bodies,[50] to take counsel with Eleasar.[51] Our Lord Jesus Christ did not permit John the Baptist to perform a miracle while still in the flesh, although He bore witness that 'among them that are born of women there hath not arisen a greater'[52] than he. Our Lord wished Peter to revere the wisdom of Paul, although Peter, by the revelation of God the Father, had recognized Him and had been given the keys of the kingdom of heaven.[53] Our Lord also allowed John, His best-loved disciple, to become so terrified that he did not dare to enter the place where His sepulchre was, although weak women often visited it.[54]

As the Scriptures say: 'To him that hath shall be given.'[55] Those who know the source of the little which they have, are successful. He who does not know whence his talents come, or, if he does know, has failed to be duly grateful to the Giver of these gifts, has lost all. This man was standing beside the most glorious Emperor, as if he were close in his confidence, when, all of a sudden, he disappeared. The unconquered Emperor Charlemagne was astonished at this unprecedented and incredible occurrence. He signed himself with the cross of our Lord and then discovered, on the spot where the man had stood, what looked like a noisome piece of coal, which had just stopped smouldering.

§34. My mention of the long cloak which the Emperor Charlemagne wore when he went out at night brings me now to his clothing in time of war. The dress and equipment of the Old Franks was as follows.[56] Their boots were gilded on the outside and decorated with leather laces more than four feet long. The wrappings round their legs were scarlet. Underneath these they wore linen garments on their legs and thighs, of the same colour, but with elaborate embroidery. Long leather thongs were cross-gartered over these wrappings and linen garments, in and out, in front and behind. Next came a white linen shirt,[57] round which was buckled a sword-belt. The sword itself was encased first in a sheath, then in a leather holder and finally in a bright white linen cover which was hardened with shining wax, so that protection was given to the middle of the leg when men drew their swords to kill people.

The last item of their clothing was a cloak, either white or blue, in the shape of a double square. This was so arranged that, when it was placed over the shoulders, it reached to the feet in front and behind, but hardly came down to the knees at the sides. In the right hand they carried a stick of apple-wood, a strong and formidable weapon, remarkable for its even knots, with a handle of gold or silver, worked with decorative engravings. I am a lazy man myself, more sluggish than a tortoise, and I have never travelled to the land of the Franks, but I saw Charles III, the King of the Franks, in full regalia, in the monastery of Saint Gall.[58] Two gold-petalled flowers stuck out from his thighs. The first of these rose up so high that it was as tall as the King himself; the second, growing gradually upwards, adorned the top of his trunk with great glory and protected him as he walked.

When the Franks, in their wars with the Gauls, saw these latter resplendent in their short striped cloaks, as happens so often in human fashion they were delighted with this novelty. They abandoned their ancient customs and began to imitate their enemies. For a time the Emperor did not forbid this dress, although he was a strict man, for it seemed more suited for fighting in battle. Later on he noticed that the Frisians were abusing the freedom he had permitted, for he caught them selling these little short cloaks at the same price as the large ones. He then gave orders that at this price no one should purchase from them any but the bigger cloaks, which were at once very broad and very long. 'What is the use of these little napkins?' he asked. 'I can't cover myself with them in bed. When I am on horseback I can't protect myself from the winds and the rain. When I go off to empty my bowels, I catch cold because my backside is frozen.'

*

In the preface to this little book, I promised that I would follow only three authorities. Werinbert, the most important of these, died seven days ago, and this very day, the thirtieth of May, we, his bereaved sons and disciples, must pay tribute to his memory.[59] Here then I bring to an end my short treatise on the piety of our Lord Charlemagne and his care of the church, which is based on the reminiscences of that priest.

The next book, which tells of the wars fought by the Emperor Charlemagne with such ferocity, is taken from the tales told by Adalbert,[60] who was the father of the same Werinbert. Adalbert was present with his master Kerold in the fighting against the Huns,[61] the Saxons and the Slavs. When I was a child, he was already a very old man. He brought me up and used to tell me about these events. I was a poor pupil, and I often ran away, but in the end he forced me to listen.

BOOK II

THE WARS AND THE MILITARY EXPLOITS
OF CHARLEMAGNE

§1. I propose to base the remainder of my story on an account given to me by a man who was not in orders and who had little experience of book-learning. It therefore seems a good idea for me to remind my readers at this point of a few facts about our forefathers, as they are recorded by painstaking historians.

When Julian the Apostate, who was hateful in the eyes of God, was killed in the Persian war by a blow aimed from heaven, not only did certain provinces across the sea secede from the Roman Empire, but so also did lands much nearer home, such as Pannonia, Noricum and Rhaetia, Germany, that is to say, and the territory of the Franks and Gauls. Next the kings of the Gauls or Franks began to decline in power: it was they who were responsible for the death of Saint Didier, Bishop of Vienne,[62] and who had expelled Columban and Gall, two most holy missionaries from across the sea. Then it was that the people called Huns first developed the habit of foraging in France and Aquitaine, in the lands, that is, of the Gauls and the Spaniards. In the end they put into the field all their forces and thus devastated the entire area, like some great fire which rages far and wide. Any objects which remained undestroyed they carried off to their impregnable hiding-places.

I have told you about Adalbert. I now explain to you the layout of these hiding-places, just as he used to describe them to me.[63] 'The land of the Huns,' he would say, 'used to be encircled by nine rings.' I could think only of wattle fences, and so I asked him: 'What in the name of goodness, sir, do you mean by that?' 'It was fortified by nine hedges,' answered he. Again I could conjure up in my mind hedges of no other kind than those which grow round our cornfields, so I questioned him once more about what he had said. 'One single ring was as wide, that is to say it contained as much territory within it, as there is land between Tours and Constance. It was built of logs of oak, beech and fir. It was twenty feet wide from edge to edge, and it was the same height. All the space inside was filled in with hard stones and heavy clay. The top of these ramparts was covered with great sods of earth. Small trees were planted within the ring, and when these were lopped and trained to bend forwards, as we often see done, they presented an impenetrable screen of twigs and foliage. Between these ramparts, hamlets and farmsteads were arranged in such a way that the human voice could carry from one to the other. Opposite the buildings little exits, which were not very big or wide, were cut into these impregnable walls, and through these exits not only those who lived on the perimeter but also people from a long way farther inside used to rush out on thieving expeditions. From the second ring, which was built exactly like the first, to the third one, stretched some twenty Teutonic miles, that is some forty Italian miles. So it continued to the ninth, although, of course, each consecutive ring was considerably smaller than the previous one. Between circle and circle all farms and habitations were laid out in such a way that the news of any happening could be conveyed from one to the other by simply blowing a trumpet.'

For two hundred years and more the Huns who swarmed there had gathered together within their fortifications the wealth of the nations of the western world. At the same time the Goths and the Vandals were busy shattering the peace of mortal beings and between them they were reducing the western world to a desert. Then in eight years the peerless

Charlemagne so tamed them that he allowed hardly any traces of them to remain.[64] As far as the Bulgars were concerned he did not press things to a final conclusion: for, once the Huns were virtually destroyed, these Bulgars did not seem likely to do much harm to the Franks. All the booty which Charlemagne discovered in the district called Pannonia he distributed with great lavishness between his bishoprics and monasteries.[65]

§2. In the war against the Saxons, in which Charlemagne was himself engaged for some considerable time,[66] two individuals not directly in the Emperor's service, whose names I would tell you if it were not for the fact that I do not wish to draw undue attention to them, organized a storming party and with great determination set about destroying the walls of a very strong city and its rampart. Charlemagne, who was most just in all his dealings, observed this. With the consent of Kerold, who was the man's master, he made the first of them commander from the Rhine to the Italian Alps, and he greatly enriched the second with grants of land.

§3. On the same occasion the sons of two of Charlemagne's nobles, whose duty it was to guard the entrance to the King's tent, lay there dead to the world one night, as a result of the drink which they had guzzled. Charlemagne, who, according to his custom, was unceasingly vigilant, went the rounds of the camp and then quietly returned to his tent without anybody recognizing him. The next morning he called all the leaders of his realm to him and asked what punishment ought to be meted out to a man who had betrayed the leader of the Franks into the hands of the enemy. The two nobles whom I mentioned at the beginning were completely unaware of what had happened; and they proffered it as their opinion that such a man should be condemned to death. Charlemagne gave the young men a wigging and then let them go unharmed.

§4. At the same place there were present two bastards, born in a brothel in Burgundy,[67] who fought most bravely in the war. The Emperor asked them who they were and where they had been born. When he learned the truth, he called them to his tent one noontide and said: 'My good fellows, I want you to serve me, and no one else.' They swore that they had come for this very purpose and that they were prepared to work for him in even the most humble capacity. 'You must serve in my chamber,' he answered. They concealed their indignation and said that they would be glad to do so. As soon as the Emperor began to drop off to sleep they seized their moment, made their way to the enemy's camp, started a fight there and washed away the taint of servitude either in their own blood or in that of their adversaries.

§5. In the midst of such preoccupations as these the magnanimous Emperor did not interrupt his habit of sending frequent messengers to carry letters and gifts to the kings of far distant regions; and from them in return came back to him whatever honours their various lands had to offer.[68] From the scene of the war with the Saxons Charlemagne sent messengers to the King of Constantinople. The latter asked the envoys if the kingdom of his son Charles was at peace, or if it was being invaded by neighbouring peoples. The leader of the envoys replied that peace reigned everywhere, except for the fact that a certain race called the Saxons were disturbing the lands of the Franks by frequent raids. 'Indeed?' said this man, who was so sluggish with sloth that he was completely useless when it came to a fight. 'Why should my son bother himself with so petty an enemy, who lacks valour and is quite devoid of fame? See, I give you the Saxon race, and everything which belongs to it.' The envoy travelled back to the warlike Charlemagne and delivered this message. The latter smiled and answered: 'The King would have done you a greater kindness if he had given you a single linen wrap to tie around your leg on the long journey home!'

§6. I must tell you about a wise answer which the same envoy gave during his visit to Greece.[69] In the Autumn he came with his fellow messengers to one of the towns which at that time belonged to the King. The party divided up and he himself was given accommodation with a certain bishop. The bishop spent all his time in fasting and prayers, and he mortified the flesh of the envoy by never giving him anything to eat. As soon as the warmer Spring weather began to bring something of a smile to the land, the bishop handed his guest over to the King. The King asked the envoy what he thought of the bishop. The envoy sighed from the very depths of his being and answered: 'That bishop is as holy as a man can be without having any conception of God.' The King was amazed. 'How can any man be holy without a knowledge of God?' he asked. The envoy replied: 'God is love; but this man is completely lacking in love.'

The King then invited the envoy to have a meal with him and placed him at table among his nobles. There was a law among these people that no one at the King's table, whether a native of the country or a visitor from foreign parts, should turn over any animal or piece of animal flesh: he must eat from the upper part as it was placed before him and from that alone. The guest did not know of their local custom, and he turned the fish over. Thereupon the nobles sprang to their feet and said to the King: 'My Lord, you are dishonoured by what has happened, as none of your ancestors was ever dishonoured before!' The King groaned and said to the envoy: 'I cannot resist what they say. You must be put to death immediately. Ask me a favour, anything you like, and I will grant it.' The envoy thought for a while, and then, with everyone listening, he said: 'My Lord Emperor, I beg of you that, in accordance with your promise, you grant me one small boon.' 'Ask whatever you wish,' said the King, 'and I will grant it: except that I cannot give you your life, for that is against the law of the Greeks.' 'I who am about to die,' answered the envoy, 'beg just this one thing of you. It is that anyone who saw me turn that fish over should have his eyes put out.' The King was dumbfounded at such a request; but he swore by Christ that he had not seen it happen himself and that all the same he believed those who had reported it to him. Next the Queen began to excuse herself. 'By Holy Mary, the blessed Mother of God,' said she, 'I myself saw nothing at all.' In their desire to escape this peril all the noblemen present then did everything in their power to free themselves from so terrible a fate. One after another they swore a terrible oath, one by the Keeper of the Keys of Heaven, another by the Apostle of the Gentiles, and the rest of them by the virtues of the Angelic Host and by the company of all the Saints. The empty-headed sons of Hellas were beaten in their own land, and the clever Frank who had worsted them came back home safe and sound.

A few years later the indefatigable Charlemagne dispatched one of his bishops to Greece, a person remarkable for his mental and physical gifts. As companion to this bishop the Emperor sent Count Hugo,[70] who was of most noble birth. These two were subjected to every possible delay and in the end they were summoned to the King's presence with their clothes in tatters. Then they were packed off on a visit to all sorts of obscure places. Eventually they were given permission to leave and they made their way home, having spent vast sums on their maintenance and their sea passage.

A short time afterwards the same King sent his own envoys to the glorious Charlemagne. By chance it happened that at this very moment the bishop and the count whom I have mentioned were staying with the Emperor. When it was announced that the envoys were about to arrive, these two advised the prudent Charlemagne that they should be conducted by a circuitous route through the mountains and pathless wildernesses, until everything which they possessed was worn out and used up. Not until they were reduced to great penury were they to be summoned to the Emperor's presence.

When the envoys finally arrived, the bishop and his fellow conspirator ordered the official in charge of the stables to sit on a lofty throne in the midst of his ostlers, in such pomp that it was impossible to believe that he was anyone else but the Emperor. The moment the envoys saw him, they fell to the ground and wanted to worship him. They were driven back by the court officials and forced to move on again. They came to another spot and there they saw the Count of the Palace in the middle of a group of noblemen who were holding council. Again they thought that it was the Emperor and they threw themselves on the ground. Those who were present said: 'That is not the Emperor! That is not the Emperor!' and hit them to compel them to move on. They went a little farther, and then they saw the Master of the King's Table, with his uniformed staff about him: and a third time they fell to the ground, imagining that this must be the Emperor. They were driven on once more until they came upon the Emperor's domestic servants, grouped in his private apartments, with the steward in their midst, and they had no doubt whatsoever that this man was the greatest of all mortals. The steward denied that he was anything of the sort; but he promised that he would use his influence with the nobles of the palace to ensure that the envoys should come into the presence of the august Emperor, if it should prove possible.

At long last there came servants direct from the Emperor's own presence, with instructions to introduce the envoys in an honourable way.

Charlemagne, of all kings the most glorious, was standing by a window through which the sun shone with dazzling brightness. He was clad in gold and precious stones, and he glittered himself like the sun at its first rising. He rested his arm upon Heito, for that was the name of the Bishop who some time previously had been sent to Constantinople.[71] Around the Emperor, like the host of heaven,[72] stood his three sons,[73] the young men who were later to share the

Empire; his daughters and their mother, adorned with wisdom, beauty and ropes of pearls; his bishops, unsurpassed in their virtue and their dignified posture, and his abbots, distinguished by their sanctity and their noble demeanour; his leaders, like Joshua when he appeared in the camp of Gilgal;[74] and his army like that which drove back the Syrians and the Assyrians out of Samaria.[75] Had David been in their midst he would have had every reason to sing: 'Kings of the earth, and all people; princes, and all judges of the earth; both young men and maidens; old men, and children: let them praise the name of the Lord.'[76] The envoys of the Greeks were dumbfounded. Their courage deserted them and they did not know which way to turn. Speechless and senseless they fell to the ground. In his great kindness the Emperor picked them up and tried to revive them with consoling words. They regained control of themselves: then they saw Heito, the man they had despised and rejected, who now stood before them in the highest honour, and they were once more filled with terror and grovelled on the ground. Charlemagne then swore to them by the King of Heaven that he would do them no harm. They took heart at this promise and began to behave with a little more confidence. In the end they went back home and never returned to our land again.

It needs to be stressed at this point that the illustrious Charlemagne employed men of the greatest ability at all levels of his service.

§7. Eight days after Epiphany, when morning lauds had been celebrated in the presence of the Emperor, these Greek envoys secretly sang to God, in their own language, certain responses which had the same chant and subject matter as *Veterem hominem* and what comes after it.[77] The Emperor thereupon ordered one of his chaplains, who had some knowledge of the Greek language, to translate these responses into Latin, with the same chant, and to take special care that every phrase corresponded precisely to the individual notes of that chant, so that, as far as the nature of the two languages permitted, the new version should in no way be dissimilar to the original one. The result is that all the words in the new version have the same phrasing as those in the old, and that in one phrase *conteruit* is found to have been substituted for *contrivit*.

These same Greek envoys brought with them every kind of organ, as well as all sorts of other instruments. These were all examined by the craftsmen of the most sagacious Charlemagne to see just what was new about them. Then the craftsmen reproduced them with the greatest possible accuracy. The chief of these was that most remarkable of organs ever possessed by musicians which, when its bronze wind-chests were filled and its bellows of ox-hide blew through its pipes of bronze, equalled with its deep note the roar of thunder, and yet which, for very sweetness, could resemble the soft tinkle of a lyre or a cymbal.[78] This is, however, neither the place nor time to tell of where it was set up, how long it lasted and the way in which it was destroyed in the general cataclysm which befell the state.

§8. At the same time envoys were sent to Charlemagne by the Persians. These envoys did not know where the land of the Franks was, so that they were very pleased with themselves when they reached the coast of Italy, for they had heard much talk of Rome and knew that Charlemagne was then its overlord. They explained to the bishops, abbots and counts of Campania and Tuscany, Emilia and Liguria, Burgundy and Gaul,[79] the reason for their coming, but they were either given false information by these people, or else they were driven away. A whole year had gone by before, weary and footsore with their wandering, they finally reached Aachen and saw Charlemagne, who was well known to them for his many achievements. They came there in the last week of Lent. Their arrival was announced to Charlemagne, but he put off seeing them until Easter Eve. When that matchless person was dressed with incomparable magnificence for the most important of all festivals, he ordered his men to introduce these envoys from a people which in earlier times had appeared awe-inspiring to the whole world. Charlemagne in all his splendour seemed to them to be so much more awesome than anyone else that they might well never have seen a king or an emperor before. He received them with great kindness and granted them this privilege: that, as if they were some of his own children, they might go wherever they wished, examine anything which caught their fancy, and ask whatever questions and make whatever inquiries they wanted to. At this they jumped for joy and valued more than all the wealth of the East the opportunity of staying near him, of gazing at him and of admiring him.

They climbed up to the ambulatory which runs round the nave of the cathedral and from there they gazed down upon the clergy and the military leaders. Then they returned to the Emperor and were not able to refrain from laughing aloud because of the greatness of their joy. They clapped their hands and kept on saying: 'Until now we have seen only men of clay: now we see golden men.' Next they went up to each of Charlemagne's nobles in turn, and stood gazing with wonder at uniforms and arms which were strange to them; then they came back once more to the Emperor, who seemed more wonderful still. They passed that night and the following day, which was Easter Sunday, in church. On the Sunday, the holiest of all days, they were invited by the munificent Charles to a sumptuous banquet along with the nobles of Europe and of the Frankish Empire. There they were so struck by the strangeness of all the unaccustomed things that they rose from the table almost as hungry as they had sat down.

The morrow's morn had chased from heaven the dewy darkness . . .[80]
And now was Aurora leaving the saffron bed of Tithonus,[81]

when, lo and behold, Charlemagne, who could never endure idleness and sloth, prepared to go off into the forest grove to hunt bison and wild oxen. He took the Persian envoys with him; but when they set eyes on these immense animals, they were filled with mighty dread, and they turned and ran. Our hero Charlemagne, on the contrary, knew no fear: sitting astride his spirited horse, he rode up to one of the beasts, drew his sword and tried to cut off its head. His blow was not successful. The huge beast ripped the Emperor's Gallic boot and leg-wrap and pinked his skin with the point of its horn, making him a little slower on foot than he had been. Maddened by the wound which had failed to kill it, the animal fled into the shelter of a coombe, which dropped abruptly down through boulders and forest trees. Almost all Charlemagne's attendants wanted to take off their riding-boots and give them to their Lord, but he refused them. 'I must go to Hildigard[82] in this state,' said he. Isembard,[83] the son of Warin, that same Warin who persecuted Othmar,[84] your own patron saint, rode after the wild beast. He did not dare to come too close, but he hurled his spear and pierced the creature to the heart between the shoulder and the windpipe, and brought it still palpitating to the Emperor. Charlemagne seemed not to have noticed what had happened. He gave the carcase to his comrades and went off home. He summoned the Queen, showed her his torn leg-wrappings and asked: 'What does the man deserve who freed me from an enemy who did this to me?' 'The greatest boon you can think of,' replied Hildigard. The Emperor then told her the entire story, point by point. The enormous horns were brought in, as proof of his story: and the Empress sighed and wept and beat her breast. When she heard that it was Isembard who was hated so much and who had been deprived of all his lands, she threw herself at the Emperor's feet and persuaded him to make full restitution of everything which had been taken from him. In addition Isembard was given a great sum of money.

These same Persian envoys brought the Emperor an elephant,[85] some monkeys, balsam, nard, unguents of various

sorts, spices, scents and a wide variety of medicaments.[86]
They seemed to have despoiled the East so that they might
offer all these gifts to the West. They soon came to be on very
familiar terms with the Emperor. One day, when they were
rather over-heated with strong beer[87] and were more merry
than usual, they said jokingly to Charlemagne, who, as
always, was calm and sober: 'Emperor, your power is indeed
great, yet it is much less than the report of it which is spread
throughout the kingdoms of the East.' When he heard this,
Charlemagne concealed his deep displeasure. He asked them
gaily enough: 'Why do you say that, my children? How has
that idea come into your heads?' They then went back to the
beginning of their story and told him all that had happened
to them since they had landed after their sea journey. 'We
Persians,' said they, 'and the Medes, Armenians, Indians,
Parthians, Elamites and all the peoples of the East, fear you
much more than we do our own ruler Harun. As for the
Macedonians and all the Greeks, what can we say of them?
They dread your overwhelming greatness more than they
fear the waves of the Ionian Sea. The inhabitants of all the
islands through which we passed on our journey were as
ready and keen to obey you as if they had been brought up
in your palace and loaded by you with immense favours. On
the other hand, or so it seems to us, the nobles of your own
territories have little respect for you, except when they are
actually in your presence. When we came to them as strangers
and asked that for love of you they should show us some
human kindness, and when we explained that we were trying
to find our way to you, they gave us no help at all but sent us
empty away.' The Emperor then deprived all the counts and
abbots, through whose lands the envoys had travelled, of
every honour which they held, and he fined the bishops an
enormous sum of money. He ordered the envoys themselves
to be conducted back to their homeland in honour and with
every care.

§9. Envoys also came to Charlemagne from the King of the Africans.[88] They brought with them a Marmarican lion, a bear from Numidia, purple dye-stuffs from Spain[89] and from Tyre the dye of the murex, together with other remarkable products of those same regions. Charlemagne, who was the most liberal of monarchs, knew that the King of Africa and all his Libyan subjects were constantly oppressed by poverty. At this time and, indeed, throughout his life, he subsidized them from the riches of Europe, and sent them vast quantities of corn, wine and oil. In this way he kept them subject to him and constantly loyal. What is more, he received a far from negligible tribute from them.[90]

Soon after this the indefatigable Emperor sent a gift of Spanish horses and mules to the ruler of the Persians. He also sent some cloaks from Frisia, white, grey, crimson and sapphire-blue, for these, so he discovered, were in short supply in those parts and extremely expensive. In addition he sent some dogs specially chosen for their nimbleness and ferocity, for these the Emperor of Persia had asked for particularly, as he needed them for hunting and warding off lions and tigers. The Persian monarch cast a careless eye over the other presents, but he made a special point of asking the envoys what wild beasts and animals these dogs were accustomed to hunt. He was told that they would immediately tear to pieces any creature to which they were set. 'Experience will show,' said he. The very next day there was heard a great shouting of shepherds, who were running away from a lion which they had seen. This din penetrated the King's palace and he said to the envoys: 'My Frankish friends, mount your horses and follow me.' The Franks eagerly set off after the King, as if they had never been tired or weary in their lives. When they came in sight of the lion, although indeed it was still a long way off, the Satrap of Satraps said to them: 'Set your dogs on the lion.' The Franks obeyed and galloped forward at full speed. The Persian lion was captured by the

German dogs, and then the envoys killed it with their swords of northern metal which had been tempered in the blood of the Saxons.

At this sight, Harun, the most powerful of all the rulers who inherited that name, recognized from such minute indications the superior might of Charlemagne, and he began to praise him in the following words: 'Now I realize that what I have heard of my brother Charles is true. By going hunting so frequently, and by exercising his mind and body with such unremitting zeal, he has acquired the habit of conquering everything under heaven. What can I offer him in return that is worthy of him, seeing that he has gone to such trouble to honour me?[91] If I give him the land which was promised to Abraham and shown to Joshua,[92] it is so far away that he cannot defend it from the barbarians. If, with his customary courage, he tries to defend it, I am afraid that the provinces bordering on the Kingdom of the Franks may secede from his Empire. All the same I will try to show my gratitude for his generosity in the way which I have said. I will give the land to him, so that he may hold it. I myself will rule over it as his representative. Whenever he wishes and whenever the opportunity offers, he may send his envoys to me. He will find me a most faithful steward of the revenues of that province.'

In this way there came to pass what the poet has described as an impossibility:

> Sooner shall Parthian exile drink the Arar
> Or Germany the Tigris.[93]

Through the energetic measures taken by Charlemagne, who was, as always, full of vigour, it was discovered to be not only possible but, indeed, extremely easy for his envoys to travel to and fro; and Harun's own messengers, both young and old, passed freely backwards and forwards from Parthia to Germany, and from Germany to Parthia – whatever interpretation philologists may put on the River Arar, some thinking it to be a tributary of the Rhine and the others of the Rhône, for, in their ignorance, they have become confused about this locality. I will call upon the whole of Germany to bear witness to this event: for in the times of your most glorious father Lewis the population of the whole country was forced to pay a penny tax for every acre of land[94] in their legal possession. This money was a contribution towards the freeing of Christians who lived in the Holy Land. In their utter misery they begged for it, in view of the former dominion exercised over them by your great-grandfather Charles and by your grandfather Lewis the Pious.

§10. An opportunity is now given me of making some honourable mention of your father, who can never be praised enough. I should like to recall some prophetic words which Charlemagne in his great wisdom said about him. When he was six years old, having spent that period being brought up with extreme care in his father's house, he was considered with some justification to be wiser than men of about sixty. His indulgent father, who hardly thought it possible that he would be able to arrange an audience for the boy with his grandfather, nevertheless took him from his mother, who had reared him with tender care, and began to instruct him how gravely and modestly he should behave in Charlemagne's presence, and how, if he were perchance asked a question, he should reply to the Emperor and show deference to his father. Eventually he took the boy into the palace. On the first or second day the Emperor observed him with interest, as he stood among the other courtiers. He said to his son: 'Who is that little boy?' Lewis the Pious answered: 'He is mine, my Lord, and yours too, if you deign to take him.' 'Bring him to me,' said Charlemagne. This was done. His serene Highness kissed the little boy and then sent him back to where he had been standing. Now that the boy knew his own rank, he scorned to be placed lower than anyone after

the Emperor himself. Very calmly and at the same time very
gracefully he moved up to stand on equal terms at his father's
side. Charlemagne, who was extremely observant, noticed this.
He called his son Lewis the Pious to him and ordered him to
discover the boy's family name, why he was acting in this
way and what made him bold enough to claim equality with
his father.[95] The boy gave the following answer, which was
reasonable enough: 'When I was your inferior, I stood behind you, among my fellow soldiers, as was proper. Now that
I am your comrade and your fellow soldier, I claim equality
with you, and I have every right to do so.' When Lewis the
Pious repeated this to the Emperor, the latter expressed himself as follows: 'If that little boy lives, he will be someone
great.' I have adapted these words from the *Life of Saint Ambrose*, for the exact words of Charlemagne cannot be translated
literally into Latin.[96] I have not gone far wrong in adapting
to Lewis the German a prophecy made about Saint Ambrose,
for Lewis closely resembled the Saint, except in certain acts
and occupations without which life on this earth cannot
be carried on, for example marriage and the use of weapons.
In his powerful leadership and even in his zeal for religion
Lewis was, if I may say so, somewhat superior to Ambrose.
In faith Lewis the German was a Catholic, devoted to the
worship of God, and a tireless comrade, protector and defender of those who served God.

Here is an instance of what I mean. When his faithful servant Hartmut, then Abbot of our own house, and now your
hermit,[97] reported to him that the tiny endowment of Saint
Gall, which had been collected together not from royal gifts
but from the small legacies left by private individuals, enjoyed none of the privileges of other monasteries and none of
the laws common to all peoples, with the result that it could
find no one to act as its defender or advocate, Lewis took a
stand against all our adversaries and was not ashamed to
champion the low esteem in which we stood, and this in the

presence of all his nobles. Without delay he wrote a letter to
you in person to say that, through your authority, once we
had taken a vote about it, we should have the right to petition
for whatsoever we wanted.[98] – Alas! What a stupid man I
am! I have been led into this digression by my own personal
gratitude and by the very special kindness which Lewis
showed to our house, and so I have forgotten just how general
his ineffable goodness was and I have given no impression of
his greatness and magnanimity.

§11. Now Lewis the German, King and Emperor of all
Germany, of Rhaetia, ancient Frankland, Saxony, Thuringia,
Noricum, Pannonia and of all the nations of the North, was a
man of large stature and noble presence. His eyes were as
bright as the stars and his voice was clear and manly. He was
remarkable for his wisdom. He relied upon an intelligence
which was naturally extremely acute, and to this he added
unceasingly by his tireless study of the Scriptures. One of his
strongest points was the extraordinary quickness with which
he anticipated and overcame the plots of his enemies, brought
to an end the quarrels of his own subjects and procured every
kind of advantage for those who were faithful to him. To all
the heathen peoples gathered round his kingdom he came to
be a terror greater than any of his predecessors. This reputation was deserved: for he never broke his word in judgement
or fouled his hands with the shedding of Christian blood,
except on one occasion, and that was one of final necessity.[99]
I dare not tell that story until I see some little Lewis or
Charles standing at your side.[100] After that one massacre,
nothing could induce him to condemn anyone else to death.
It was his habit to inflict the following punishments upon
those found guilty of disloyalty and plotting: he simply deprived them of their offices, and never, in any circumstance
whatsoever, or after any passage of time, did he so soften his
heart that he would permit them to return to their former
rank.

Lewis the German surpassed all men in his zealous devotion to prayer, in his observance of the fasts and in his constant care to attend divine service. He followed the example of Saint Martin in that, whatever else he was doing, he always seemed to pray to God as if he were face to face with him.[101] On the days ordained he abstained from meat and from dainty food. Whenever the litanies were to be used he would follow the cross barefoot from his palace as far as the cathedral.[102] If he were in Ratisbon he would walk barefoot as far as Saint Emmeram's.[103] In other towns he accepted the habits of those he was with. He built new churches of wonderful workmanship in Frankfurt and Ratisbon. In this latter place there was a shortage of stones with which to complete the immense fabric, and so Lewis the German ordered the city walls to be torn down. In holes in these walls he discovered the bones of men long since dead wrapped around with so much gold that not only was he able to decorate the cathedral with it, but he also covered entire books, which were copied subsequently, with bindings nearly an inch thick made of the same material. No churchman could stay in his service or even come into his presence unless he were skilled at reading and chanting. He despised monks who broke their vow, and he had the warmest affection for those who kept it. He was always so full of mirth and good temper that if anyone came to him in a melancholic mood, after just looking at him and exchanging a few words with him they went away happy. If by chance anything evil or stupid occurred when he was present, or if he heard of such a thing happening elsewhere, a single glance of his eyes was sufficient to put all right again, so that what is written of the eternal Judge, who sees into our hearts, might fairly be said to have some first beginnings in him, beyond what can rightly be granted to mortal men: 'A king that sitteth on the throne of judgement, scattereth away all evil with his eyes.'[104]

I have written this as a short digression. If I live to do it and if God is willing, I promise to write more about Lewis the German.

§12. Now I must return to my subject. While the Emperor Charlemagne was being detained rather too long in Aachen by the arrival of visitors and by the hostility of the unconquered Saxons, or by the depredations and piracy first of the Northmen and then of the Moors,[105] and while the war against the Huns was being waged by his son Pepin,[106] barbarous peoples who came from the North ravaged a great part of Noricum and eastern Frankland. When this was reported to Charlemagne, he subdued them himself. He ordered all their boys and children to be measured by the sword, that is, any who exceeded such a measurement were shortened by a head.[107]

This incident led eventually to another, which was more important and more serious.[108] When your Imperial Majesty's holy grandfather departed this life, certain giants, like those which Scripture tells us were, through God's anger, begotten by the sons of Seth from the daughters of Cain, blown up with the spirit of pride and doubtless like those others who asked: 'What part have we in David and what inheritance in the son of Jesse?'[109] these men, I say, despised the children of Charlemagne for their virtuous behaviour, and each in turn tried to seize for himself the command of the kingdom and to place the crown on his own head. Then by the inspiration of God certain other men from the lower classes protested that, just as the famous Emperor Charlemagne had once measured the enemies of Christendom with the sword, so, if only one of his descendants could be found as tall as a sword, then he ought to rule over the Franks and over the whole of Germany. The devilish faction of conspirators was scattered far and wide, just as if it had been struck by a thunderbolt.

Charlemagne was victorious over his foreign foes, but he was threatened by his own people in a remarkable conspiracy which came to nothing in the end. On his return to Ratisbon from the war against the Slavs,[110] he was nearly captured and put to death by his own son, the child of one of his mistresses, who had been given by his mother the ill-omened name of the glorious Pepin. The plot was revealed in the following way. This man Pepin had been planning the death of the Emperor with a group of nobles in the church of Saint Peter. When their meeting was over, Pepin, who was afraid of every shadow, ordered a search to be made, in case there was any-one hidden in the corners or beneath the altars. Lo and behold, just as they feared, they found a cleric hidden under the altar. When they had captured him, they made him swear that he would not betray their conspiracy. To save his life he dared not refuse to swear the oath which they dictated. Once they were gone, he no longer considered himself bound by his oath and he hurried off to the palace. With the greatest pos-sible difficulty, he passed through all the seven gateways which were barred against him, and came in the end to the Emperor's chamber. He knocked on the door, thus causing great astonishment to the ever-wakeful Charlemagne, who wondered who it could possibly be who was disturbing him at that hour of night. Charlemagne ordered the womenfolk, who travelled with him to look after the Queen and her daughters, to go out to see who was at the door and what he wanted. They went out and found the wretched cleric. They barred the doors again, and, with much laughter and chatter-ing, pulled their skirts over their faces and tried to hide in the corners. The Emperor, who was no fool and whom nothing under heaven could escape, questioned the women closely to find what was wrong with them and who had knocked at the door. When he learned that it was only some beardless boy, out of his wits and probably mad, dressed in a linen surplice, with pants underneath, who was asking to speak with him immediately, Charlemagne ordered the man to be admitted. The cleric fell at the Emperor's feet and revealed all that had happened, point by point. All the conspirators, who suspected nothing, were dealt with as they deserved before the third hour of the day, some being sent into exile and others being punished. Pepin himself, who was a dwarf and a hunchback, was given a sound whipping and was tonsured. As a punishment he was sent for some time to the monastery of Saint Gall, that being among the poorest and most austere of all places in the far-flung Empire.

A short time later some of the Frankish leaders planned to lay hands on their King. This was well known to Charlemagne and yet he was unwilling to destroy them, for, if only they had been loyal, they might have been a great source of protection to all Christian men. He sent messengers to Pepin to ask what ought to be done about these conspirators. The messengers found Pepin in the garden with the older brethren, for the younger men were busy with more serious occupations. He was digging up nettles and weeds with a three-pronged hoe, so that more useful plants could grow there without obstruction. They told him why they had come. Pepin sighed deeply from the bottom of his heart, for all deformed people have a tendency to be more irritable than those who are properly proportioned, and said in reply: 'If Charlemagne had thought my advice worth having, he would not treat me so harshly. I have no advice to give. Tell him just this: what you have found me doing.' The messengers were afraid to go back to the formidable Emperor without a proper answer. Again and again they asked Pepin what message they should carry back to their master. In the end he lost his temper. 'I send him no message at all, except what I am doing. I am digging up useless weeds, so that useful vegetables may grow more freely.'[111]

The messengers went off sadly, thinking that they had nothing rational to report. When they came to the Emperor and were asked what answer they brought, they replied that after so much effort and travelling they were not a wit wiser. The King, who was a very intelligent man, asked them point by point where they had found Pepin, what he was doing and what answer he had given them. 'We found him sitting on a rustic seat and turning over the earth of a vegetable garden with a hoe,' said they. 'We told him the reason for our journey, but, although we questioned him repeatedly, we could extract no other answer but this: "I send him no message at all," he said, "except what I am doing. I am digging up useless weeds, so that useful vegetables may grow more freely."' When he heard this, the Emperor, who was not lacking in perspicacity and who was a very wise man, rubbed his ears and breathed heavily through his nose. 'My good servants,' said he, 'you have brought back a most sensible reply.' The messengers were afraid that they stood in peril of their lives, but Charlemagne was able to divine the true meaning of Pepin's words. He removed all these conspirators from the land of the living, and gave to his loyal supporters the room to grow and spread which had been occupied by these useless men. One of his enemies, who had chosen as his reward the highest hill in the land of the Franks and all the land which he could see from the hilltop, he ordered to be hanged from a high gallows on that very same hill. He told his bastard Pepin to choose the way of life which pleased him most. When this permission was given, Pepin chose a place in the most noble monastery then in existence.[112] It is now destroyed, and the manner of its destruction is only too well known. I will not describe its end, until I see your little son Bernard with a sword girt to his thigh.[113]

The noble Charlemagne was often angry because he was obliged to go out and fight against barbarous peoples when one of his leaders seemed well suited to the task. This I can prove from the action of a man who came from my own neighbourhood. He was a man called Eishere,[114] from the Thurgau, who, as his name implies, formed 'a large part of a terrifying army'. He was so tall that you would have thought that he was descended from the race of Anak, if these last had not lived so far away and so long ago.[115] Whenever he came to the River Thur, swollen and foaming with mountain torrents, and was unable to force his great horse into the stream, which was more like solid ice than flowing water, he would seize the reins and force his horse to swim behind him, saying: 'By Saint Gall, you must follow me, whether you want to or not!' This man marched with the Emperor in his troop of soldiers, and mowed down the Bohemians and Wiltzes and Avars as a man mows a meadow. He spitted them on his spear as if they were tiny birds. When he came back victorious, the stay-at-homes asked him how he liked it in the land of the Winides. Contemptuous of some and angry with others, he used to answer: 'What were these tadpoles to me? I used to spit seven, or eight, or sometimes nine of them on my spear, and carry them about all over the place, squealing their incomprehensible lingo. The King my master and I ought never to have worn ourselves out fighting such worms.'

§13. At about this time, when the Emperor was just completing his campaign against the Huns and had received the surrender of the peoples whom I have just mentioned, the Northmen started their invasion and began to cause great anxiety to the Gauls and the Franks. The unconquerable Charlemagne turned back and strove to invade them in their own homes, marching overland through a hostile and trackless countryside. Either the will of God held him back, so that, as the Scripture says, 'He might make trial of Israel',[116] or else our own sins stood in the way, for all his efforts ended in frustration. In a single night, for example, to the great discomfort of the whole army, fifty pairs of oxen belonging to a single abbot, died of a sudden attack of pest.[117] Charlemagne, who was the wisest of men, decided to abandon his plan, preferring not to disobey Scripture by 'trying to move against the current of the stream'. At a moment when Charlemagne was travelling on a protracted journey across his own wide Empire, Godefrid, the King of the Northmen, encouraged by the Emperor's absence, invaded the territory of the Frankish kingdom and settled down in the neighbourhood of the Moselle.[118] Godefrid's own son, whose mother the King had only recently repudiated, so that he might marry another woman in her place, caught up with him just as he was calling his falcon off a heron, and cut him through the middle with his sword. Then, just as happened long ago when Holofernes was slain,[119] none of the Northmen dared to rely any longer upon his courage or his weapons, but all sought safety in flight. In this way the land of the Franks was liberated without any great effort being made, and no one could boast to God as the ungrateful Israel had done.[120] The unconquered and unconquerable Charlemagne gave thanks to God for His decision, but he complained bitterly because some of the Northmen had escaped through his absence. 'I am greatly saddened,' said he, 'that I have not been thought worthy to let my Christian hand sport with these dog-heads.'

§14.   Once when he was on a journey Charlemagne came unheralded to a certain town which lies on the seashore in Southern Gaul. While he sat eating his supper incognito, a raiding-party of Northmen made a piratical attack on the harbour of this town. As their ships came in sight, some said that they were Jewish merchants, others that they were Africans or traders from Britain. Charlemagne in his wisdom knew better. From the build of the ships and their speed through the water he recognized them as enemies rather than merchants. 'Those ships are not loaded with goods,' he said to his men. 'They are filled with savage enemies.' When they heard this, they rushed off to the ships at full speed, each striving to be the first to reach them. They were not successful. As soon as the Northmen learned that the man whom they were accustomed to call Charles the Hammer was in the neighbourhood, they sailed away at incredible speed.[121] They were not content with avoiding the swords of the pursuers; they were determined to hurry out of sight, too, for fear that their whole fleet might be driven back, or even destroyed and broken up into small pieces. Charlemagne, who was a God-fearing, just and devout ruler, rose from the table and stood at a window facing east. For a long time the precious tears poured down his face. No one dared to ask him why. In the end he explained his lachrymose behaviour to his war-like leaders. 'My faithful servants,' said he, 'do you know why I wept so bitterly? I am not afraid that these ruffians will be able to do me any harm; but I am sick at heart to think that even in my lifetime they have dared to attack this coast, and I am horror-stricken when I foresee what evil they will do to my descendants and their subjects.'

May the protection of Christ our Lord prevent this from ever coming to pass! May your own sword, tempered already in the gore of the Nordostrani, stand in their way; and may the sword of your brother Carloman, which is stained in their blood, too, be joined to yours.[122] Carloman's sword is now rusting away, not through cowardice, but for want of funds and because the lands of your most faithful Arnulf are so circumscribed.[123] If you in your mighty power only have the will to ordain this, it should not be a difficult matter for this sword to be made sharp and bright once more. This one small bough, together with the tiny twig which is Bernard,[124] is all that is left to burgeon on the once prolific stock of Lewis the Pious, and it is under the branch of your own protection, which alone remains, that it is free to form its leaf.

Let me at this point insert into the history of your namesake Charles a story of your great-great-grandfather Pepin, so that, if God in His clemency so wills it, some future little Charles or some tiny Lewis yet unborn may come to emulate it.

§15. At a time when the Longobards and their other enemies were attacking them, the inhabitants of Rome sent messengers to Pepin to beg that, for Saint Peter's sake, he should deign to come to their help with all possible speed.[125] In due course Pepin subdued their enemies and, as soon as he had won this victory, entered Rome so that he might pray there.[126] He was received by the Romans with this song of praise: 'Today there have met together the fellow citizens of the Apostles and those who serve God, to bring concord and glory to their own homeland, and to give peace to the Gentiles and freedom to the Lord's own people.' Those who are unaware of the meaning and the origin of this song have developed the habit of singing it on the birthdays of the Apostles. Pepin was afraid of the ill-will of the Romans, and even more so of the inhabitants of Constantinople, and he soon returned home to the land of the Franks.

Pepin discovered that the leaders of his army were in the habit of speaking contemptuously of him in private. He ordered a bull of fantastic size and ferocious temper to be set free.[127] Then a savage lion was set at the bull. With tremendous fury the lion charged at the bull, seized it by the neck and hurled it to the ground. The King said to those standing round him: 'Now drag the lion off the bull, or else kill it on top of its enemy.' They looked at each other in terror, with their hearts frozen with fear, and just managed to gasp out an answer. 'My Lord,' they muttered, 'there is no man under heaven who would dare to attempt such a thing.' Pepin rose without hesitation from his throne, drew his sword, and cut through the lion's neck and severed the bull's head from its shoulders. Then he sheathed his sword and sat down once more on his throne. 'Do you think that I am worthy to be your master?' asked he. 'Have you not heard what the diminutive David did to the huge Goliath? Or what tiny Alexander did to his noblemen?' They fell to the ground as if they had been struck by thunder. 'Is there anyone so foolish that he would deny your right to rule over the whole of mankind?' they replied.

Not only was Pepin master over beasts and men, but he also fought an incredible battle against the powers of evil. The thermal baths had not yet been built at Aachen; but the healing springs boiled forth there with great heat. Pepin ordered his personal servant to make sure that the springs were clean and that no stranger had been permitted to enter. When this was done the King took his sword in his hand and marched off for a bath in his shirt and slippers. Suddenly the Old Enemy came to meet him and made as if to kill him. The King protected himself with the sign of the Cross and drew his sword. He perceived a shape in human form. With his unconquerable sword he struck through it into the ground, in such a way that it was only after a long struggle that he managed with great difficulty to draw the sword out again. All the same, the shape had such substance to it that it befouled all the neighbouring springs with blood and gore and horrid slime. The irrepressible Pepin was in no way abashed by this. 'Take no notice of what has happened,' said he to his servant. 'Let the dirty water run for a while. As soon as it begins to come clear again, then I will have my bath at once.'

§16. I had originally intended, noble Emperor, to limit my short history to your great-grandfather Charlemagne, all of whose deeds are well known to you. Since the opportunity inevitably arose for mention to be made of your glorious father Lewis the German, and then of your devout grandfather Lewis the Pious of holy memory, and finally of your warlike great-great-grandfather, the younger Pepin, concerning all of whom very little has been recorded, thanks to the crass laziness of my contemporaries, I thought that it would be wrong to leave them out. To this King Pepin the learned Bede has devoted almost an entire book of his *Ecclesiastical History*.[128] Now that I have set down all these stories by way of digression, I must return, as smoothly as any swan may swim, to your illustrious namesake Charles. If I do not leave out some of his warlike deeds, I shall never come to consider his daily habits. I will now tell you, as briefly as I know how, such incidents as occur to me.

§17. Once the unconquerable Pepin was dead, the Longobards began again to harass Rome. Charlemagne who, like his father, was never beaten in battle, was fully occupied to the north of the Alps, but he marched swiftly into Italy. After a bloodless campaign, the Longobards were sufficiently humbled to surrender of their own free will and Charlemagne received them into subjection. For security's sake and to stop them ever again seceding from Frankish rule or doing harm to the territories of Saint Peter, Charlemagne married the daughter of Desiderius, King of the Longobards.[129] Some short time afterwards, since she was bedridden and unable to bear a child, she was, by the advice of his devout clergy, put on one side as if already dead. Her father was furious. He bound his neighbours to him by oath, shut himself up within the walls of Pavia and prepared to do battle with the invincible Charlemagne. As soon as he had made sure that this was true, Charlemagne hurried with all speed to Pavia.

Now it had happened some years earlier that one of Charlemagne's principal nobles, Otker by name, had incurred the wrath of the formidable Emperor and had therefore fled to this same Desiderius.[130] When they heard that the dreaded Charlemagne was coming near, these too went up into a high tower from which they could see anyone approaching from far and wide. As soon as the baggage trains came into sight, moving even more quickly than those of Darius or Julius Caesar, Desiderius said to Otker: 'Is Charles in the midst of that vast array?' 'Not yet, not yet,' answered Otker. When he perceived the army itself, collected together from all the nations of Charlemagne's vast Empire, Desiderius said sharply to Otker: 'Now Charles is advancing proudly in the midst of his troops.' 'Not yet, not yet,' answered Otker. Desiderius than flew into a panic and said: 'If even more soldiers come into battle with him, what can we possibly do?' 'When he comes,' said Otker, 'you will see what he is like. I don't know what will happen to us.' As they spoke together, the sovereign's escort appeared, tireless as ever. When he saw them Desiderius was stupefied. 'This time it really is Charles,' said he. 'Not yet, not yet,' said Otker once more. After this the bishops came into sight, and the abbots and the clergy of Charlemagne's chapel, with their attendants. When he saw them Desiderius longed for death and began to hate the light of day. With a sob in his voice he stammered: 'Let us go down and hide ourselves in the earth, in the face of the fury of an enemy so terrible.' Otker, too, was terrified, for in happier days he had been in close contact with the strategy and the military equipment of the peerless Charlemagne, and he knew all about them. 'When you see the fields bristle as with ears of iron corn,' he said, 'when you see the Po and the Ticino break over the walls of your city in great waves which gleam black with the glint of iron, then indeed you can be sure that Charlemagne is at hand.' He had not yet finished his words when from the west a mighty gale and with it the wind of the true north began to blow up like some great pall of cloud, which turned the bright daylight into frightful gloom. As the Emperor rode on and ever on, from the gleam of his weapons dawned as it were another day, more dark than any night for the beleaguered force.

Then came in sight that man of iron, Charlemagne, topped with his iron helm, his fists in iron gloves, his iron chest and his Platonic shoulders clad in an iron cuirass. An iron spear raised high against the sky he gripped in his left hand, while in his right he held his still unconquered sword. For greater ease of riding other men keep their thighs bare of armour; Charlemagne's were bound in plates of iron. As for his greaves, like those of all his army, they, too, were made of iron. His shield was all of iron. His horse gleamed iron-coloured and its very mettle was as if of iron. All those who rode before him, those who kept him company on either flank, those who followed after, wore the same armour, and their gear was as close a copy of his own as it is possible to imagine. Iron filled the fields and all the open spaces. The rays of the sun were thrown back by this battle-line of iron. This race of men harder than iron did homage to the very hardness of iron. The pallid face of the man in the condemned cell grew paler at the bright gleam of iron. 'Oh! the iron! alas for the iron!' Such was the confused clamour of the citizens of Pavia. The strong walls shook at the touch of iron. The resolution of the young grew feeble before the iron of these older men. When therefore Otker, who had foreseen the truth, with one swift glance observed all this, which I, a toothless man with stammering speech, have tried to describe, not as I ought, but slowly and with labyrinthine phrase, he said to Desiderius: 'That is Charlemagne, whom you have sought so long.' As he spoke he fell half conscious to the ground.

The inhabitants of the city, either through madness or because they had some hope of resisting, refused to let Charlemagne enter on that day. The ingenious Emperor therefore said to his men: 'Let us today construct something memorable, so that we may not be accused of passing the day in idleness. Let us make haste to build a little house of prayer, in which, if they do not soon throw open the gates to us, we may devote ourselves to the service of God.' As soon as he had said this, his men hurried off to collect lime and stones, with wood and paint, and brought them to the workmen who always accompanied him. Between the fourth hour of the day and the twelfth, with the help of the leaders and the common soldiery, they had built such a cathedral, with walls and roofs, panelled ceilings and painted frescoes, that no one watching would have believed that it could have been achieved in a whole year. How, on the following day, some of the citizens wanted to open the gates to him, others wished to resist him, hopeless as it seemed, and yet others chose to shut themselves up, and how Charlemagne, with great ease, without any shedding of blood, but simply by his military skill, conquered and captured the city, all this I leave for others to tell, for those who follow your Highness not for love but in the hope of gain.[131]

Charlemagne, the most devout of Emperors, soon turned his attention to other matters. He came to the city of Friuli, which pedants call Forojuliensis. It happened that, just at that time, the bishop of the city, or, to use the modern expression, the patriarch, was drawing near to the end of his life. The pious Charlemagne made haste to visit him, so that the bishop might nominate his own successor. However, that holy man sighed from the bottom of his heart and said: 'My Lord, I leave to the judgement of God and to your own decision this bishopric which I have occupied for such a long time without being of use or spiritual advantage to anyone. I, who am on the point of death, am unwilling to add to the mountain of sins which I have accumulated during my life anything more for which I shall have to answer before the unavoidable and incorruptible Judge.' When the wise Charlemagne heard this, he rightly decided that the bishop was worthy to be compared with the early fathers.

When Charlemagne, that most energetic of all the bustling Franks, had stayed for some time in this neighbourhood, occupied with the appointment of a worthy successor to the dying bishop, he said to his men one festal day, after the celebration of Mass: 'Let us go hunting and see what we can catch. We must not become lazy and sluggish, or give way to idleness. We can all set out in the clothes which we are wearing at this moment.' The day was cold and overclouded. Charlemagne himself was wearing a sheepskin, which had not cost more than the cope of Saint Martin, which he is said to have wrapped round his chest, leaving his arms bare, when he was offering to God a sacrifice which received divine approval.[132] It was carnival time and the others had just come from Pavia, to which city the Venetians had of late brought from their lands beyond the sea all the riches of the East. They strutted forth in pheasant skins sewn on to silk, or in the neck and back and tail feathers of peacocks just coming into full plumage. Some were decked out in ribbons of Tyrian purple and of lemon colour; others were wrapped around with skins of ermine. As they rushed through the woodland gullies, they were lacerated by the branches of trees and thorns and briars, they were drenched with rain and they were befouled with the blood of wild beasts and with the stench of the skins. In such a state as this they returned home. 'None of us must take off the skins before bedtime,' said the cunning Charlemagne. 'It is much better that they should dry on us.' By now they were more interested in their physical welfare than in the state of their garments, and, at this command, they rushed to the fires and did all they could to warm themselves. Soon Charlemagne called them back and they were kept dancing attendance until late into the night. Finally they were dismissed to their quarters. When at last they began to take off their delicate skin garments and their even more delicate girdles, the splitting of their creased and shrunken finery could be heard from far away, like the snapping of twigs in the dry season. They groaned and they sighed and they complained when they thought of how much money they had wasted in a single day. They had received an order from the Emperor to appear in the same skins the next morning. When they came they were no longer resplendent in these garments of theirs. On the contrary they looked squalid in their stained and muddy tatters. Charlemagne bustled about and said to his servant: 'Give that sheepskin of mine a rub between your fingers and then bring it in for me to look at.' It was carried in, snow-white and in perfect condition. Charlemagne took it in his hands and held it up before the crowd standing around. 'What fools you all are!' he said. 'Which of these skins is the more valuable and the more useful, this of mine which cost a single piece of gold, or those of yours which you bought for pounds and pounds, or maybe even for hundreds and hundreds of pounds?' At this they all looked down at the ground, for they could not bear this terrible censure.

Your own father, who was a very strict man, imitated this example not just once or twice, but throughout the whole of his life. When with his army and on a campaign against the enemy, he never allowed anyone whom he considered worthy of his attention or his training to wear anything except his military equipment over garments of wool and linen. If any of his retainers, unaware of this ruling of his, happened by chance to meet him with silk or gold or silver on his person, he would receive this reprimand and would depart a better and a wiser man: 'What are you dolled up in gold, silver and scarlet for? You poor miserable wretch! Aren't you satisfied with dying yourself in battle, if that is to be your fate? Must you also hand over your worldly goods to the enemy? You might have ransomed your soul with them, instead of which they will go to adorn the idols of the heathen!' I tell you this, you who know it better than I do, that from his earliest youth until his seventieth year the unconquered Lewis always wore iron for preference, and what a figure he made before the envoys of the Northmen when he stood there clad in iron!

§18. When the Kings of the Northmen each sent him gold and silver, as a proof of their loyalty, and their own swords, as a mark of their perpetual subjection and surrender, Lewis the German ordered the money to be thrown on the ground, to be sneered at by everyone and to be trodden underfoot as if it were dirt. He ordered the swords, on the other hand, to be passed to him where he sat on his lofty throne, so that he could test them himself. The envoys were anxious that no suspicion of treachery should be levelled against them, and they handed the swords to the Emperor by the point, at their own peril, as servants hand knives to their masters. Lewis took one of them by the hilt and tried to bend it from its tip to its handle. His hands were stronger than the sword, and the blade snapped. Then one of the envoys drew his own sword from its sheath and handed it to Lewis as a servant would do, so that he might test that. 'My Lord,' said he, 'I think that you will find this sword as flexible and strong as your own victorious hand could wish.' The Emperor took the sword. He was an Emperor indeed! As the prophet Isaiah said in his prophecy: 'Look unto the rock whence ye are hewn!'[133] For he, alone out of all the vast population of Germany, by the grace of God rose in strength and courage to the level of our forefathers. He bent the sword like a vine-twig, from the extreme tip back to the hilt, and then let it gradually straighten out again. The envoys gazed at each other in amazement and muttered among themselves: 'If only gold and silver were held as cheap by our leaders, and iron were as precious!'

§19. As I am writing about the Northmen, I will show from a trifling incident which occurred in your grandfather's time how lightly those people valued religious faith and baptism.[134] Just as after the death of David, the warrior King, the neigh-bouring peoples, long held in check by his powerful hand, paid tribute to his peaceful son Solomon,[135] so this terrible race of Northmen had a similar respect for Charlemagne's son, Lewis the Pious, and in their fear paid him the tribute which they had given to that august Emperor. On one occasion the Emperor Lewis the Pious took pity on the en-voys of the Northmen and asked them if they would be willing to accept the Christian faith. They replied that they were prepared to obey him always and everywhere and in all matters. He ordered them to be baptized in the name of Him of whom the most sage Augustine says: 'If there were no Trinity the Truth would not have said: "Go and teach all peoples, baptizing them in the name of the Father, the Son and the Holy Ghost."' The nobles of the royal palace adopted these Northmen, almost as if they had been children: each received a white robe from the Emperor's wardrobe, and from his sponsors a full set of Frankish garments, with arms, costly robes and other adornments. This was done repeatedly, and more and more came each year, not for the sake of Christ but for mundane advantages. They used to hurry over on Easter Eve to pay homage to the Emperor, more like faithful vassals than foreign envoys. On one occasion as many as fifty arrived. The Emperor asked them if they wished to be baptized. When they had confessed their sins, he ordered them to be sprinkled with holy water. As there were not enough linen garments to go round on that occasion, Lewis ordered some old shirts[136] to be cut up and to be tacked together to make tunics[137] or to be run up as overalls.[138] When one of these without more ado was put on a certain elderly envoy, he regarded it suspiciously for some time. Then he lost control of himself completely and said to the Emperor: 'Look here! I've gone through this ablutions business about twenty times already, and I've always been rigged out before with a splendid white suit; but this old sack makes me feel more like a pig-farmer than a soldier! If it weren't for the fact that you've pinched my own clothes and not given me any new ones, with the result that I should feel a right fool if I walked out of here naked, you could keep your Christ and your suit of reach-me-downs, too!'[139]

How little do the enemies of Christ value the words of the Lord's Apostle when he says: 'For as many of you as have been baptized have put on Christ',[140] and again: 'So many of us as were baptized into Christ Jesus were baptized into His death,'[141] or that passage which is aimed particularly at those who despise the faith and violate the sacraments: 'Crucifying the Son of God afresh and putting Him to an open shame.'[142] If only this were the case with the Gentiles merely, instead of being found so frequently in those who are called by the name of Christ!

§20. Now I must tell you a story about the kindliness of the first Lewis, and then I will return to Charlemagne. Lewis the Pious was a most peaceful Emperor, for he did not know what it was to be attacked by hostile forces. He was therefore free to devote all his energy to work of religion, prayer, charitable activities, listening to lawsuits and making just legal decisions. He had a natural genius for this kind of business and with long practice he became even better. One day a man who was considered by everyone to be a veritable Achitophel tried to deceive him. As Lewis replied his face seemed friendly enough and his voice was very kindly, but he was somewhat upset all the same. 'You are very clever, Anselm,' said the Emperor, 'but, if I might be allowed to say so, I would venture to point out that you are deviating from the path of truth.' From that day forward this legal luminary lost any reputation which he may have had in anybody's eyes.

§21. Lewis the Pious, who was a very kindly man, was so preoccupied with his various charitable activities that he preferred to see them done with his own eyes, if not actually to do them with his own hands. Above all, he made special arrangements for the trial of poor people, against the occasions when he himself should be absent. He ordered that cases concerning the poor should be tried before one of their own number, a man of broken-down physique but who apparently possessed more spirit than the others. This man was put in charge of the restoration of stolen property, retaliation in kind for injuries and wounds received, and, in more serious cases, the cutting off of limbs, decapitations and the public display of those executed. Heads of departments, tribunes of the people, leaders of each hundred and their representatives were all appointed, but this man pressed on regardless with the task which had been entrusted to him.

The Emperor himself was so open-handed that he was never weary of giving food and clothing to the poor, for he worshipped Christ in their persons. This he did especially on the day when Christ left His mortal body and prepared to assume His incorruptible one. On that day he gave presents to each and every one who served in the palace or was a member of the royal household. To the more noble of their number he would order sword-belts to be distributed, or leg-wraps or the more expensive items of clothing fetched from the farthest confines of the Empire. To the lower ranks Frisian cloaks of every hue would be handed out. The grooms, bakers of bread and cooks were given linen garments, lengths of woollen cloth or sheath knives, according to what they said they needed. Once 'there was none among them that lacked',[143] as it says in the Acts of the Apostles, then everyone was filled with gratitude. The poor, until recently in rags and tatters, but now rejoicing in their new-found cleanliness, would raise their voices to the heavens, as they wandered through the great courtyard and the arcades of Aachen, or the porticoes, as the Romans call them, and shout 'Kyrie Eleison to the blessed Lewis!' Such of the soldiers as could manage it would kiss the Emperor's feet, and others would worship him from afar as he walked in procession to church. On one of these occasions, a court jester said facetiously: 'Happy art thou, Lewis, who hath clothed so many men on one day. By Christ, no one in the whole length and breadth of Europe has clad more people than you, except, of course, the man Atto.' Lewis asked the fool how Atto had managed to clothe even more people, but he, delighted at having secured the Emperor's attention, merely replied, with a bellow of laughter: 'Atto has given away more clothes today.' Lewis the Pious, with a most kindly expression still on his face, took this for the silly joke which it was, and proceeded humbly and devoutly in to church. Once inside he behaved with such reverence that he seemed to see the Lord Jesus Christ standing before him.

Every Saturday Lewis used to go to the baths, not that he had any need to, but because it gave him an opportunity of distributing gifts. Everything which he took off, except his sword and sword-belt, he would give away to his attendants. He was liberal even to the most humble of people. He once ordered all his clothing to be handed over to the glazier Stracholf, one of the workmen from Saint Gall, who was waiting on him at the time. When the vagabond batmen of the Emperor's soldiery heard of this, they lay in wait for Stracholf and tried to rob him. 'What do you think you are doing?' shouted Stracholf. 'You are laying hands on the Emperor's own glazier!' 'You can keep your lordly office,' said they, 'but . . .'

NOTES

NOTES TO THE INTRODUCTION

*Full bibliographical details can be found in the
Bibliography on pages 201–2.*

1. cf. *Charlemagne*, by the Monk of Saint Gall, Bk. II, §12 (p. 153).
2. See map on page 43.
3. *The Life of Charlemagne*, by Einhard, §25 (p. 79).
4. ibid.
5. H. W. C. Davis, *Charlemagne, the Hero of Two Nations*, 1899, edition of 1925, p. 169.
6. H. W. Garrod, *Einhard's Life of Charlemagne*, 1915, p. xli.
7. *The Life of Charlemagne*, by Einhard, §29 (p. 82).
8. *The Age of Charlemagne*, D. Bullough, 1965.
9. It is clear from the wording that Walahfrid Strabo wrote his prologue after Einhard's death in 840. He himself died in 849, so that the prologue was composed at some time in that decade.
10. See Walahfrid Strabo's prologue, p. 49. See also the *Epitaphium Einhardi*, written by Rhabanus Maurus, Abbot of Fulda (822–42), where Einhard is called '*vir nobilis*' (v, 3).
11. See Walahfrid Strabo's prologue, p. 49. The date of Einhard's birth is not known. By inference it was *c.* 770, for he was sent to study at Fulda after 779 and he died in 840.
12. Rhabanus Maurus, *Epitaphium Einhardi*, v, 4.
13. She and her husband are named as benefactors in one of the eighth-century manuscripts in the Monastery of Fulda: '*Ego Einhart et coniux mea Engilfrit donamus et tradimus ... quicquid in Urithorpfe proprietatis habemus ...*'
14. See Walahfrid Strabo's prologue, p. 49.
15. ibid. p. 49.
16. *Ep. ad regem* 85: '*Beseleel, vester immo et noster familiaris adiutor ...*'

cf. Exodus, XXXI, 2–5: 'See, I have called by name Bezaleel the son of Uri, the son of Hur, of the tribe of Judah: and I have filled him with the spirit of God, in wisdom, and in understanding, and in knowledge, and in all manner of workmanship, to devise cunning works, to work in gold, and in silver, and in brass, and in cutting of stones, to set them, and in carving of timber, to work in all manner of workmanship.' Thomas Hodgkin wrote of Einhard that '... he seems to have held a position in Charles's cabinet like that of a modern First Commissioner of Works ...', *Italy and her Invaders, 744–774*, Vol. VII, 1899, p. 293. In Vol. VIII, p. 136, of the same work, Hodgkin gives a list of twenty of these nicknames used at Charlemagne's court. Louis Halphen refuses to accept most of this, '*Einhard, historien de Charlemagne*', Ch. III of *Études critiques sur l'histoire de Charlemagne*, 1921, pp. 73–6.

17. *De Einharto Magno*, vv, 1–3:

> *Nec minor est magni reverentia patris habenda*
> *Beseleel, faber primum qui percepit omne*
> *Artificum precautus opus ...*

18. '... *exactor operum regalium in Aquisgrani palatio regio sub Heinhardo abbate ...*' *Gesta abbatum Fontanellensium* in G. H. Pertz, *Monumenta Germaniae Historica*, Vol. II, p. 293.

19. '... *ad Einhartum varıarum artium doctorem peritissimum ...* *Catalogus abbatum Fuldensium*, III, p. 162.

20. *Carmen 242*, vv, 7–8:

> *Sic regit ipse domum totam sibi Nardulus istam.*
> '*Nardule*', *dic lector pergens:* '*tu parvule, salve*'.

21. ibid. vv, 4–6:

> *Mel apis egregium portat tibi corpore parvo.*
> *Parva quidem res est oculorum, cerne, pupilla;*
> *Sed regit imperio vivacis corporis actus.*

22. *Carmina Theodulfi*, III, 1, vv, 155–6:

> *Nardulus, huc illuc di currat perpete gressu,*
> *Ut, formica, tuus pes redit itque frequens.*

23. See his prologue, p. 50.

24. A document of Lewis the Pious, dated 815, is the first to refer to

this marriage: '... *fideli nostro Einhardo nec non et coniugi suae Immae*', Codex Laureshamensis, I, 44.

25. This date is much debated. In a catalogue of manuscripts possessed by the monks of Reichenau a copy is listed under 'the eighth year of the reign of the Emperor Lewis', that is Lewis the Pious, i.e. 821; but this entry is now thought to be a later addition, made after the death of Einhard. Louis Halphen goes so far as to suggest that the Reichenau manuscript was in reality the one divided into chapters by Walahfrid Strabo, and to which he added his prologue, between 840 and 849, when he was Abbot of that house. (See Louis Halphen, *Eginhard. Vie de Charlemagne, éditée et traduite par L.H., Classiques de l'Histoire de France au Moyen Age*, 3rd edition, 1947, p. viii, n. 1.)

26. op cit. in n. 25, p. vii.

27. ibid. pp. vii–viii, for this and the following details. See also the same author, op. cit. in n. 16, p. 81, etc.

28. These are the opening sentences on Pepin the Short in §§2 and 15, the details given about Hildigard in §18 and about the mother of Pepin the Hunchback in §20 and the statement concerning Charlemagne's command of the Latin language in §25.

29. It is known that Rotrude had an illegitimate son Lewis, later Abbot of Saint Denis, and that Bertha had several illegitimate children.

30. '*815 Jan. 11, Aquisgrani palatio regio. Einhartus et eius coniux Imma a Ludovico I imperatore locum Michlinstat in silva Odenewalt et villam Mulinheim superiorem in pago Moynecgowe dono accipiunt.*' Diploma Ludovici, Codex Laureshamensis, I, 44.

31. Louis Halphen, op. cit. in n. 16, plays down all this. Just as he sees little or no proof of Einhard's artistic skills in the quotations given in nn. 18, 19, etc., so he maintains that the mission to Leo III was not important, and that Einhard's role in the events of 813 was greatly exaggerated by later writers, e.g. Ermoldus Nigellus in his poem *In honorem Hludowici*.

32. op. cit. in n. 6, p. xxvi.

33. '*Grâce à cette méthode, il a été à même d'écrire une oeuvre très nettement supérieure au point de vue de la forme à tout ce que le moyen âge occidental avait jusqu'alors produit en ce genre. Qu'on compare cette biographie bien ordonnée, en dépit de quelques gaucheries, d'un style ferme*

et relativement correct, aux vies de saints antérieures, et l'on mesure le chemin parcouru.' op. cit. in n. 25, p. xii.

34. ibid. p. xi.

35. Philipp Jaffé, *Einharti vita Caroli*, preface, p. 501, n. 2, p. 502, n. 1 and p. 503, n. 1, in *Bibliotheca Rerum Germanicarum*, Vol. IV, *Monumenta Carolina*, 1867, reprinted 1964.

36. H. W. Garrod, op. cit. in n. 6, p. xxix.

37. A. J. Grant, *Early Lives of Charlemagne by Eginhard and the Monk of Saint Gall*, 1922, p. xvi.

38. H. W. Garrod, op. cit. in n. 6, p. xxxii.

39. op. cit. in n. 25, p. xiii. For all that, Louis Halphen is a severe critic of Einhard. His chapter entitled *'Einhard, historien de Charlemagne'*, in *Etudes critiques sur l'histoire de Charlemagne*, 1921, pp. 60–103, sets out to establish that *'qu'on semble même avoir jusqu'ici beaucoup exagéré l'importance du témoignage d'Einhard comme historien de Charlemagne'* (p. 61).

40. Bk. II, §17, pp. 162–5.

41. H. W. C. Davis translates the passage, op. cit. in n. 5, pp. 79–80. When travelling in Lombardy in 1856, Lord Macaulay turned part of the Monk's account into verse:

Paraphrase

To Oggier spake King Didier:
'When cometh Charlemagne?
We looked for him in harvest:
We looked for him in rain.
Crops are reaped; and floods are past;
And still he is not here.
Some token show, that we may know
That Charlemagne is near.'

Then to the King made answer
Oggier, the christened Dane:
'When stands the iron harvest
Ripe on the Lombard plain,
That stiff harvest which is reaped
With sword of knight and peer,
Then by that sign ye may divine
That Charlemagne is near.

> 'When round the Lombard cities
> The iron flood shall flow,
> A swifter flood than Ticin,
> A broader flood than Po,
> Frothing white with many a plume,
> Dark blue with many a spear,
> Then by that sign ye may divine
> That Charlemagne is near.'

This part of the story of the siege of Pavia Macaulay had taken from Sir Anthony Panizzi, *Essay on the Romantic Narrative Poetry of the Italians*, prefixed to his edition of Boiardo's *Orlando Innamorato* and Ariosto's *Orlando Furioso*, 1830–34, Vol. I, p. 123, n. *b*, where Panizzi quotes a few lines from the Monk of Saint Gall in Latin and asks: 'Is not this evidently taken from poetical effusions?' Thomas Hodgkin, *Italy and her Invaders*, Vol. VII, pp. 381–3, also gives a partial translation.

42. Bk. I, §10, p. 104. A small but interesting detail is that when, after quoting Virgil, the Monk wants to say that rumour, from being as small as a tomtit, grows to be as big as an eagle, he says that '*fama . . . de minima meisa super aquilarum magnitudinem excresceret*', using a Latinized form of the Old High German *meise*, the root of the Modern French *mésange* (Bk. I, §25, p. 121).

43. Bk. II, §12, p. 156. Eishere was from the Thurgau and he came from the Monk's own neighbourhood.

44. Bk. I, §34, p. 134. Kerold was killed in 799.

45. Bk. I, §34, p. 133. Werinbert is mentioned elsewhere, in the *Liber Evangeliorum* of the poet Otfrid of Weissenburg. He is known to have died in 884.

46. Bk. I, §9, p. 101.

47. Bk. II, §10, p. 150. Hartmut became Abbot in 872, on the death of Grimald, and he resigned on 6 December 883.

48. Bk. I, §30, p. 128.

49. Bk. I, §34, p. 133.

50. Bk. I, §31, p. 129.

51. Bk. II, §12, p. 156.

52. Bk. I, §10, p. 104.

53. Bk. II, §12, p. 155.

54. Bk. II, §12, p. 156.

55. Bk. II, §10, p. 150.

56. Bk. I, §10, p. 104.

57. Bk. I, §29, p. 126.

58. Bk. II, §12, p. 156.

59. Bk. II, §21, p. 172.

60. Ratpert, author of the first part of the *Casus Sancti Galli*, quoted in G. H. Pertz, *Monumenta Germaniae Historica, Scriptores*, II, 74: '... *contigit domnum imperatorem de Italia redeuntem nostrum intrare monasterium; ... ipse enim laetus triduo ibidem permansit.*'

61. Bk. I, 34, p. 133. We are a far cry from Charlemagne, his linen leg-wraps and his sheepskin coat.

62. Bk. I, §18, p. 110 and p. 111; Bk. II, §10, p. 149; and Bk. II, §14, p. 159.

63. cf. n. 60.

64. See '*Casus Sancti Galli*', in G. H. Pertz, *Monumenta Germaniae Historica, Scriptores*, Vol. II, p. 94: '*Notker corpore non animo gracilis, voce non spiritu balbulus* ...'; he goes on: '*In orando, legendo, dictando, creberrimus* ...'

65. '*Le Moine de Saint-Gall*', Ch. IV of *Etudes critiques sur l'histoire de Charlemagne*, pp. 139–42.

66. *Monumenta Germaniae, Legés*, Vol. V: *Formulae Merowingici et Carolini Aevi*, ed. G. H. Pertz, 1882, p. 412.

67. P. von Winterfeld, '*Notkers Vita S. Galli*', in *Neues Archiv der Gesellschaft für ältere deutsche Geschichtskunde*, Vol. XXVII, 1902, p. 748.

68. Philipp Jaffé, *Monachus Sangallensis De Carolo Magno*, p. 628, in *Bibliotheca Rerum Germanicarum*, Vol. VI, *Monumenta Carolina*, Berlin, 1867, reprinted 1964: '*Fabula ut nullo tempore abest a rebus gestis hominum* ...; *monachus* ... *hon tam sincerae rerum veterum historiae gnarus quam iucundis narratiunculis salsisque dictis refertus.*'

69. op. cit. in n. 37, p. xxii.

70. op. cit. in n. 6, p. xxxi. In the eighteenth century Dom Bouqet, *Recueil des historiens des Gaules et de la France*, Vol. V, 1744, p. x, had been even more scathing: '*Il est inutile de nous mettre en peine davantage d'en rechercher l'auteur: car l'ouvrage le déshonore plus qu'il ne l'honore* ...'

71. A. Kleinclausz, *Charlemagne*, 1934, p. xxxii.

72. op. cit. in n. 65, p. 106.

73. There is a brief mention in V, 10–11. Contrast the Monk of Saint Gall, Bk. II, §16, p. 161: 'To the elder Pepin the most learned Bede has devoted almost an entire book of his *Ecclesiastical History*.'

74. MS. Hanover XIII, 858 calls the *Vita Caroli* of Einhard and the annals attributed to Einhard '*liber primus gestorum Karoli*'; and the two books by the Monk of Saint Gall form the second and third books of these '*gesta Karoli*'.

75. Bk. I, §34, p. 133: '... *hic fiat terminus libelli istius ... de religiositate et aecclesiastica domni Karoli cura ...*'

76. Bk. I, §34, p. 133: '*Sequens vero (libellus) de bellicis rebus acerrimi Karoli ...*'

77. Bk. II, §16, p. 161: '... *cottidianam eius conversationem ...*' It is possible that the Monk meant to squeeze this into Book II. On the other hand, Bk. II, §21, ends in mid-sentence, and it is possible that Book III once existed.

78. Bk. I, §18, p. 110.

79. Bk. I, §34, p. 134.

80. Bk. II, §1, p. 135.

81. Bk. II, §2, p. 137.

82. Bk. II, §12, pp. 156–7.

83. *The Life of Charlemagne*, §20, p. 75.

84. Bk. II, §12, pp. 155–6. If the way in which it is inserted into the chapter is odd, the story is well told. A. J. Grant is wrong to call it a 'story, which is here told somewhat clumsily' (op. cit. in n. 37, p. 174).

85. Bk. II, §17, p. 163. Platonic shoulders, '*humerosque Platonicos*', seems to be a play on Plato's name, from πλατος, breadth, width. In his book, *Charlemagne, the Hero of Two Nations* (see n. 5), pp. 79–80, H. W. C. Davis translated part of this passage by the Monk and then added a footnote: 'This saga is translated into Latin by the Monk of Saint Gall ...' Which saga Davis wanted to pretend that he himself was translating he does not explain.

86. cf. no. 40.

87. King Charles rides on in great anger. His white beard lay outside his cuirass. All the French leaders spur on their horses at full speed. *La Chanson de Roland*, ll. 1842–4.

88. See Bk. I, §31, p. 129; Bk. II, §8, p. 144; Bk. I, §25, p. 121; Bk. II, §8, p. 144; and Bk. II, §9, p. 148.

89. See Bk. II, §16, p. 161 and Bk. II, §12, p. 155.

90. Bk. I, §28, p. 126. Cf. *Georgics*, I, 472–3:

> *Vidimus undantem ruptis fornacibus Aetnam*
> *Flammarunque globos liquefactaque volvere saxa!*

91. Bk. II, §6, p. 141. Cf. Acts 7, 42; or Deuteronomy 17, 3.

92. Bk. II, §9, p. 147. Cf. *Aeneid*, IX, 582:

> *Pictus acu chlamydem, et ferrugine clarus Ibera.*

93. Bk. II, §10, p. 150.

94. Bk. II, §11, p. 152, and Bk. II, §17, p. 165.

95. Bk. I, §3, p. 95.

96. Bk. II, §17, p. 166.

97. Bk. I, §34, p. 133.

98. See Louis Halphen, op. cit. in n. 65, pp. 106–7, n. 2, for a discussion of these three manuscripts, H, Z and N.

NOTES TO
THE LIFE OF CHARLEMAGNE
BY EINHARD

Full bibliographical details can be found in the
Bibliography on pages 201–2.

1. See pp. 16–17. The Benedictine Abbey of Fulda was founded in 744 at the instigation of Saint Boniface. Sturm was its first abbot. Baugolf was abbot 779–802.

2. These rubrics, set by Walahfrid Strabo at the head of each numbered section, are not included in editions of the text.

3. It was suggested by Louis Halphen that this introduction by Einhard may have been modelled on the preface to the *De vita Caesarum* of Suetonius, which is now lost.

4. In his early days at Aachen Einhard received instruction in the company of Charlemagne's sons and it was at this period that he began his friendship with Lewis the Pious.

5. *Tusculanae Disputationes*, I, iii, 6.

6. It was Pope Zacharias who was consulted about the deposition of

Childeric III. Pope Stephen II crowned Pepin the Short at Saint Denis in 754.

7. This cart, the *carpentum pompaticum*, like the long hair and beards of the Merovingian kings, was really a sign of their royal and religious dignity.

8. The battle of Poitiers, 732.

9. The battle on the River Berre, 737.

10. Carloman died in 755.

11. Pepin the Short died on 24 September 768.

12. Carloman, brother of Charlemagne, died in December 771. He had reigned for three years.

13. Waifar died in 768, only a short time before Pepin the Short. This Hunold was not Duke Hunold, father of Waifar, who had spent many years as a monk on the Ile de Rhé.

14. This is a gross understatement. In effect Pepin invaded Italy twice, in 754 and 756.

15. The brief war with Rotgaud, Duke of Friuli, occurred some two years after the fall of Pavia, but Einhard seems to imply that the two events followed immediately after each other. The Monk imitates Einhard in this error, for he, too, moves Charlemagne to Friuli immediately after the fall of Pavia, but for a different reason, Bk. II, §17, p. 165.

16. See p. 6 and p. 22 for details of the war against the Longobards. Desiderius remained until his death in the monastery of Corbie. The events of 773–4 form the subject of Alessandro Manzoni's tragedy *Adelchi*, first published in 1822, to which he prefixed a series of *Notizie Storiche*. See also Manzoni's long essay entitled *Discorso sopra alcuni punti della storia longobardica in Italia*, 1822, revised 1845.

17. See p. 6. The Saxon wars lasted from 772 until 804.

18. Charlemagne also met the Saxons in battle near Lübeck in 775 and at Bochult in 779.

19. The battle of Detmold, 783.

20. The battle near Osnabrück, on the River Haase, 783.

21. This is the battle of Roncevaux (so called since *La Chanson de Roland*) which took place on 15 August 778. Einhard gives no name to the action and stresses that only 'the last part of the baggage train and the troops who were marching in support of

the rearguard' were engaged. The original version of the *Annales regni Francorum*, against the date 778, had not even mentioned this reverse: '*Ibi obsides receptos de Ibn el Arabi et de Abutauro et de multis Sarracenis, Pampilona destructa, Hispani Wascones subjugatos etiam et Navarros, reversus in partibus Franciae.*' (Hostages were handed over by Ibn el Arabi, by Abou Thaur and by a number of other Saracens, Pamplona was destroyed, the Spanish Basques were beaten into subjection and so were the men of Navarre: and then Charlemagne returned to certain parts of Frankland.) The later, revised version of the *Annales regni Francorum*, which Einhard is clearly following, has a not dissimilar account, but an important new passage is included: '*Regredi statuens Pyrinei saltum ingressus est. In cuius summitate Wascones insidiis conlocatis, extremum agmen adorti, totum exercitum magno tumulto perturbant. Et licet Franci Wasconibus tam armis quam animis praestare viderentur, tamen et iniquitate locorum et genere imparis pugnae inferiores effecti sunt. In hoc certamine plerique aulicorum quos rex copiis praefecerat interfecti sunt, direpta impedimenta et hostis propter notitiam locorum statim in diversa dilapsus est.*' (He decided to turn back and marched into a pass through the Pyrenees. The Basques had placed an ambush at the top of the pass: they attacked the rearguard and threw Charlemagne's whole army into confusion. Although clearly enough the Franks were superior to the Basques by their weapons and in their courage, their superiority was nullified by the mountainous nature of the terrain and by the unfair way in which the battle was fought. In this conflict were killed most of the military leaders whom Charlemagne had put in charge of his troops, the baggage was stolen, and then without more ado the enemy, who had a most detailed knowledge of the neighbourhood, slipped away in all directions.) Writing some twenty years after the event, the unknown reviser of the *Annales regni Francorum* chose to insert this account of a conflict which had not been mentioned at all in the earlier text; the engagement was sufficiently important for him to have a clear memory of the details, unless he took them from some lost source; he maintains that the whole Frankish army was engaged; and he states clearly that many of the Frankish commanders were killed. Einhard markes two basic changes: he reduces the '*totum exercitum*' of the revised *Annales regni Francorum* to 'extremam impedimentorum partem et eos qui, novissimi agminis incedentes subsidio'; and he names three of the military leaders who were killed, Eggihard, Anshelm and Roland. There is a third description of the battle of Roncevaux. Some time after 840, the nameless author of the Vita Hludovici, called by literary historians the Limousin Astronomer, includes the following passage: 'Dum enim quae agi potuerunt in Hispania peracta essent et prospero itinere reditum esset, infortunio obviante, extremi quidam in eodem monte regii caesi sunt agminis. Quorum nomina, quia vulgata sunt, dicere supersedi.' (Once all that could be achieved had duly been accomplished in Spain, the homeward march was successfully begun. A disaster occurred on the journey, for in that same mountain range certain troops of the King's rearguard were cut to pieces. As everybody knows their names, I will not trouble to list them.) Again no names are given, but the Limousin Astronomer states clearly that they were all fresh in men's memories more than sixty years after the battle. We also possess the epitaph of Eggihard, who was Charlemagne's seneschal, cf. Monumenta Germaniae, Poetae Carolini Aevi, Vol. I, p. 109, and this gives the actual date of the Battle of Roncevaux, for we are told that Eggihard '. . . obiit die octodecima kalendas septembrias' (= 15 August) 778.

22. As explained on p. 7, this victory in 786, by Audulf, was short-lived. Wido beat the Bretons in 799, and they offered their allegiance to Charlemagne at Tours in 800; but they were once more in revolt in 811.

23. The expedition against Areghis took place in 786–7.

24. The war with Tassilo III, Duke of Bavaria, took place in 787–8. See p. 17.

25. By Huns, as always, Einhard means the Avars.

26. Duke Tassilo was forced to become a monk in the monastery of Jumièges.

27. The Baltic is some 850–900 miles in length and 100–200 miles wide.

28. This was the campaign of 789. The Wiltzes rose in rebellion again in 808.

29. In effect the war against the Avars lasted from 791 until 803.

30. The death of Eric, Duke of Friuli, in 799, was not connected with the war against the Avars.

31. The Bohemian war took place in 805.

32. The war against the Linonici, in 808, was not successful, and they rose again in 811.

33. See p. 7 for the wars against the Danes, which lasted from 804 to 810.

34. Einhard adds Aquitaine to make Charlemagne's achievements more impressive.

35. Charlemagne did not take Tortosa, and his Empire did not extend to the Ebro.

36. Einhard exaggerates by adding Calabria to the Carolingian Empire.

37. No such letters exist. One wonders if Einhard had really seen them.

38. No such letters exist. In any case, Einhard may mean Eardulf, King of Northumbria (cf. p. 7), rather than the kings of the Irish, whom he calls 'Scottorum quoque reges ...' On the other hand, Charlemagne certainly had diplomatic relations with the Irish.

39. Charlemagne sent an ambassador to the Holy Sepulchre in 799. When this ambassador returned in November 800, he brought from the Patriarch of Jerusalem, not from Harun-al-Rachid (Caliph of Bagdad, 786–809), the Keys of the Holy Sepulchre and of Mount Calvary, as a sign of deference, not as a surrender of jurisdiction. In 801 ambassadors to Charlemagne from Harun-al-Rachid landed at Pisa, and not long after arrived the elephant, Abu-l-Abbas, which lived until 810. Einhard seems to have invented the story that this was the only elephant in Harun's possession, 'quem tunc solum habebat'! It was not until 807 that a new embassy arrived from Harun-al-Rachid, with rich materials, spices, and, although Einhard does not mention them, a waterclock, candelabra and a tent. As he does so often, Einhard is misreading his prime source, the revised version of the *Annales regni Francorum*, and telescoping the details.

40. Nicephorus I was Emperor 802–811, Michael I 811–13 and Leo V 813–20. The messengers from Leo V did not arrive until after Charlemagne's death.

41. The revised *Annales regni Francorum*, which Einhard is following, include Nice, against the year 813: '*Mauri ... Centumcellas Tusciae civitatem et Niceam provinciae Narbonensis vastaverunt.*'

42. This first marriage probably took place in 770.

43. Hildigard died on 30 April 783. By her Charlemagne had four sons and four daughters, according to Paul the Deacon: one son, the twin of Lewis, called Lothar, died as a baby and is not mentioned by Einhard; two daughters, Hildigard and Adelhaid, died as babies, so that Einhard seems to err in one of his names, unless there were really five daughters.

44. Fastrada, Charlemagne's third wife, died in 794.

45. Liutgard, the fourth wife, died in 800.

46. Drogo was Archbishop of Metz from 823 to 855.

47. Hugo became Abbot of the monastery of Saint Quentin and died in 844.

48. Bertrada died on 12 July 783.

49. Gisela was Abbess of the convent of Chelles, Seine-et-Marne.

50. This omits the children who died young.

51. Charles died on 4 December 811.

52. Pepin had been King of Italy since 781. He died on 8 July 810.

53. Rotrude died on 6 June 810. She had been engaged as a child to the Emperor Constantine VI in 781. cf. p. 7.

54. Pope Hadrian I died in 796.

55. By Count Rorigo Rotrude had an illegitimate son called Lewis, who became Abbot of Saint Denis. Bertha had several illegitimate children, among them the historian Nithard, by the poet Angilbert, whom Charlemagne addressed as Homer and who later became lay Abbot of Saint Riquier near Abbeville.

56. This concubine was Himiltrude.

57. The conspiracy took place in 792.

58. This was the revolt of Hardrad in 785-6.

59. The main act of cruelty remembered against Charlemagne was the hanging of 4,500 Saxon rebels in one day at Verden in 782, and this was before his marriage with Fastrada.

60. Many of the details of this chapter, including the following one, are taken from what Suetonius had said about Caesar, Augustus, Tiberius, Claudius and Nero!

61. These doors are still to be seen in the great church at Aachen.

62. There is still in existence a letter from Pope Hadrian I in which he authorizes Charlemagne to move marbles and mosaics from the palace in Ravenna to help him with his constructions in Aachen,

Codex Carolinus, letter 67, in *Monumenta Germaniae, Epistolae Merowingici et Karolini Aevi*, Vol. I, p. 614.

63. There was only morning Mass. Charlemagne went, too, to morning, evening and late-night Hours.

64. See p. 8 for details of these four visits.

65. The attack on Leo III occurred on 25 April 799. An attempt was made to blind him and cut out his tongue; had it succeeded he would have been forced to give up all priestly offices. The Pope fled to Charlemagne's camp at Paderborn. Charlemagne came to Rome on 24 November 800. He was crowned Emperor in Saint Peter's on 25 December of that year.

66. The Emperors of Constantinople considered themselves, with justification, to be the sole heirs of the Roman Emperors. In 800 the Empress Irene ruled in Constantinople.

67. The laws of the Salian Franks and those of the Ripuarian Franks.

68. None of this remains.

69. *Wintarmanoth* = winter month.

70. *Hornung*. cf. *Hornung* (Modern German), from *Horn* (Old High German), = corner = the turn of the year.

71. *Lentzinmanoth* = renewal month. cf. Lent, in Modern English.

72. *Ostarmanoth* = Easter month.

73. *Winnemanoth* = month of joy.

74. *Brachmanoth* = month of ploughing, the breaking of the soil.

75. *Heuuimanoth* = the hay month.

76. *Aranmanoth* = the month of the corn ears.

77. *Witumanoth* = the wood month.

78. *Windumemanoth* = month of the wine harvest.

79. *Herbistmanoth* = the harvest month = *Herbstmonat* (Modern German) = September.

80. *Heilagmanoth* = Holy month.

81. Pepin had died on 8 July 810 and Charles on 4 December 811.

82. This coronation took place in the great church at Aachen on 11 September 813.

83. Einhard is following the revised version of the *Annales regni Francorum*, but, as so often, he puts the events in the wrong sequence. Charlemagne went hunting in the Ardennes in the summer of 813, fell ill, and decided as a result to crown his son Lewis.

84. This implies that Charlemagne was born in 742. In the epitaph on p. 84, I have translated *septuagenarius* as 'more than seventy years old', to agree with this; but if Einhard really means 'seventy', then he is contradicting himself and making 744 the date of birth.

85. The tomb was opened by the Emperor Otto III in 1000 and the body is supposed to have been found seated on a chair and in a good state of preservation. In 1165 the tomb was again visited, and this time the remains were found in a marble sarcophagus. A. J. Grant, *Early Lives of Charlemagne by Eginhard and the Monk of Saint Gall*, 1907, p. 169, prints a translation of the description of Otto's visit as given in the *Chronicon Novaliciense*, iii, 32: 'after the passage of many years the Emperor Otto III came into the district where the body of Charles was lying duly buried. He descended into the place of burial with two bishops and Otto, Count of Lomello; the Emperor himself completed the party of four. Now, the Count gave his version of what happened much as follows: "We came then to Charles. He was not lying down, as is usual with the bodies of the dead, but sat on a sort of seat, as though he were alive. He was crowned with a golden crown; he held his sceptre in his hands, and his hands were covered with gloves, through which his nails had forced a passage. Round him there was a sort of vault built, strongly made of mortar and marble. When we came to the grave we broke a hole into it and entered, and entering, were aware of a very strong odour. At once we fell upon our knees and worshipped him, and the Emperor Otto clothed him with white garments, cut his nails and restored whatever was lacking in him. But corruption had not yet taken anything away from his limbs; only a little was lacking to the very tip of his nose. Otto had this restored in gold; he then took a single tooth from his mouth, and so built up the vault, and departed." '

86. Einhard had read of similar portents in the *Lives* of Augustus, Caligula and Claudius, as related by Suetonius. According to the *Annales regni Francorum*, there were in the year 806–807 three eclipses of the moon, one of the sun and a spot on the sun which lasted for eight days. There was an eclipse of the moon in 809, two eclipses of the moon and two of the sun in 810 and an eclipse of the sun in 812. Einhard tidies this up!

87. The portico fell in 817, three years after Charlemagne's death.

88. cf. *supra*, §17. The bridge over the Rhine at Mainz was burned in May 813. As Einhard says, it was of wood, so that it could hardly have been expected to last for ever.

89. In 810.

90. Hildebald, Archbishop of Cologne, 785–818, who administered the last sacrament to Charlemagne.

91. Richolf, Archbishop of Mainz, 787–813.

92. Arn, Archbishop of Salzburg.

93. Wolfar, Archbishop of Rheims.

94. Bernoin, Archbishop of Clermont, *c.* 811–*c.* 823.

95. Laidrad, Archbishop of Lyons.

96. John, Archbishop of Arles.

97. Theodulf, Bishop of Orleans, 788–821.

98. Jesse, Bishop of Amiens, 799–836.

99. Heito, Bishop of Basel, 802–822, died 836.

100. Waltgaud, Bishop of Liège.

101. Fridugis, Abbot of Saint Martin de Tours.

102. Adalung, Abbot of Lorsch.

103. Engilbert, or Angilbert, Abbot of Saint Riquier, the reputed father of the illegitimate children of Bertha, daughter of Charlemagne. He died in 835.

104. Irmino, Abbot of Saint-Germain-des-Prés, 812–17.

105. Walah, later Abbot of Corbie under Lewis the Pious, *c.* 822. He died in 835.

106. Meginher: a Count Meginharius, son-in-law of the Hardrad who conspired against Charlemagne in 785–6, is mentioned in 817 in the *Annales regni Francorum*.

107. Otulf: there was a Count Audulfus in Bavaria at this time.

108. Stephen: a Count of Paris bore this name at the beginning of the ninth century.

109. Unruoc was the grandfather of the Emperor Berengarius.

110. Burchard: the name of a constable, *comes stabuli*, who is mentioned in the *Annales regni Francorum* for the years 807 and 811.

111. Meginhard: mentioned as one of the counts sent as envoys to the Danish King Hemming in 810. See p. 8.

112. Rihwin: possibly Ricouin, Count of Padua, mentioned in the *Annales regni Francorum*, *sub anno* 814.

113. Edo: possibly Count Uodo, who accompanied Meginhard on his mission in 810.

114. Gerold: possibly a count who was Lord of the Eastern Marches from *c.* 811 until 832.

115. Bero: possibly Bera, Count of Barcelona, *c.* 813.

116. Louis Halphen points out that a very different account of the scrupulousness, or lack of it, of Lewis the Pious is given both by Thegan, in his *De gestis Domini Lodewici Imperatoris*, ch. 8, and by Nithard, in *De dissensionibus filiorum Loduvici Pii*, I, 2 (see *Eginhard, Vie de Charlemagne*, p. 103).

NOTES TO
CHARLEMAGNE
BY NOTKER THE STAMMERER

*Full bibliographical details can be found in the
Bibliography on pages 201–2.*

1. From December 771 onwards, after the death of Carloman.

2. Clement and Dungal. In reality Clement the Scot came to the court of Lewis the Pious *c.* 817. Dungal was a monk in the Abbey of Saint Denis from 784 until 811, and he may be the person who was teaching in Pavia in 825.

3. The Abbey of San Pietro in Cielo d'Oro near Pavia was sometimes named after Saint Augustine, because it contained many of his relics.

4. For Alcuin see p. 10 and Einhard *The Life of Charlemagne*, p. 79. Actually, Charlemagne met Alcuin, for the second time, in Parma in 781, and persuaded him to move from there to Aachen.

5. The Monk no doubt had at his disposal the anonymous *Vita Alcuini*. The anachronism by which Alcuin, who was born *c.* 735, is made the pupil of Bede, who died in 735, is typical of his carelessness. The original text says: '*Bedae doctissimi discipulo Hecberto traditur.*' The Monk has simply omitted Egbert, whom Bede taught and who taught Alcuin!

6. As stated on p. 26, the over-use of the superlative of the adjective and the adverb was a weakness of both Notker Balbulus and the Monk of Saint Gall, if they may be considered separately. Louis

Halphen counted 20 superlatives on 3 pages of the Latin text of the *De Carolo Magno* as printed by Philipp Jaffé. Here, in a few lines, Charlemagne is 'religiosissimus' and Bede both 'doctissimus' and 'peritissimus quidem post sanctum Gregorium in scripturis tractatoris'. I have reduced many of these superlatives.

7. This passage about Saint Martin seems to be adapted from the *De exordiis et incrementis . . .* of Walahfrid Strabo, in *Monumenta Germaniae, Capitularia*, Vol. II, p. 515.

8. This is part of one of the responses for Saint Martin's Day, 11 November. The point of the story is that, confused by the words '*Fiat voluntas tua*', which come several times in these responses, the monk moved over to the Lord's Prayer, with 'Thy kingdom come' and the others had to continue 'Thy will be done'.

9. Here, as on p. 94, the Monk is following the *Vita Alcuini*: '. . . of all his pupils there was not one . . .' is his own addition.

10. According to Ekkehard IV, *Casus Sancti Galli*, in *Monumenta Germaniae Historica Scriptores*, Vol. II, pp. 78–9, the teachers of Notker the Stammerer were Moengal, an Irishman later called Marcellus, and Yso, author of the two books of the *De miraculis Sancti Otmari*, but Hartmut and Grimald are mentioned a sentence or two later. This would, in any case, be a weak point on which to establish a division between Notker and the Monk, for the Hanover MS has simply G. for *Grimaldus*, and in the Stuttgart and Wiblingen MSS even G. is omitted.

11. Grimald died in 872. Alcuin died in 804, so that it is most unlikely that he can have taught Grimald.

12. cf. p. 4. When Pope Stephen III crowned Pepin the Short, on 28 July 754, he appointed Charlemagne and Carloman as joint heirs to their father.

13. The Monk again seems to be following Walahfrid Strabo's *De exordiis et incrementis . . .*, Vol. II, p. 508.

14. Zachariah VIII, 23.

15. This *invidia* of the Greeks and Romans for the Franks is copied from Einhard, *The Life of Charlemagne*, §28, p. 81. The Monk refers to it again in Bk. I, §26 (p. 122) and a third time, with reference to Pepin the Short, in Bk. II, §15 (p. 160).

16. Drogo, son of Charlemagne by the concubine Regina (cf. Einhard, *The Life of Charlemagne*, p. 73), who was born in 801, became

Bishop of Metz in 826 and died in 855. The Monk seems to have taken much of this passage from the *Vita Gregorii Magni*, II, 9–10. The anachronism concerning Drogo, who was 13 only at Charlemagne's death, is his own invention.

17. The Monk seems to be thinking of Amalarius of Metz, *c.* 780–850, a pupil of Alcuin, who compiled a standard antiphonary and wrote the well-known treatise *Liber de ordine antiphonarii*.

18. The words 'with houses' = *massilis*, with no variant. cf. Du Cange, IV, 240, *masnilus* = house, Godefroi, V, 96a, *maisil* = house.

19. The word 'rents' = *rautinis*, with no variant. Is this a miscopying for *rantinis*? cf. Du Cange, V, 703, 585, *renta* > *ranta* (> *rantina*).

20. The wars against the Avars, whom the Monk consistently calls the Huns, lasted from 791 to 799. Hildigard had died in 783!

21. The words '. . . *non contentus episcopatu, quem in prima sede Germaniae retinet* . . .' imply Mainz. If Charlemagne was fighting the Avars, this can only mean Bishop Riculf, 787–813 (cf. Einhard, *The Life of Charlemagne*, p. 90, where he appears as Richolf), who was admirable in every way, but this is pressing the Monk too hard.

22. Charles the Fat, for whom the Monk is writing.

23. I Timothy, 3, 1.

24. The word 'beadle' = *scarionem*.

25. The word 'veltres', *velter* (obsolete English), and *veltris* (medieval Latin) = a small hunting dog.

26. The word 'quails' appears as *caras*, MS. H *quacaras*. Du Cange quotes this sentence, II, 168: *quacara, quaquila, quaquilia,* onomatopoeic forms, > *qualea, qualia,* (vulgar Latin), *quaglia* (Modern Italian), *caille* (Modern French).

27. The only bishop called Recho during the reign of Charlemagne held the see of Strasbourg, which was hardly 'a minute township'.

28. The words '. . . *Alasatiensi illo Sigultario* . . .' in Philipp Jaffé, *Monumenta Carolina*, Vol. IV, p. 652, have this note: '*vino Sigoltesheimensi*'.

29. The word 'drinking-pot' = *poticulam*; cf. p. 119, l. 32.

30. *Aeneid*, IV, 174–5, translation of C. Day Lewis, Hogarth Press, 1952.

31. The words 'as small as a tomtit' = *de minima meisa* < meisa

(Old High German), > *Meise* (Modern German), *mésange* (Modern French).

32. Matthew, 16, 18.

33. This passage is taken in all probability from the *Lorsch Annals, sub annis* 799–800. cf. Einhard, *The Life of Charlemagne*, §28, p. 81: Einhard seems to think that the attempt to blind Leo III and to cut out his tongue, made on 25 April 799, had been successful. cf. n. 65 on p. 186

34. Michael I did not become Emperor until 811!

35. This passage seems to be taken from the *Lorsch Annals, sub anno* 801.

36. This statement seems quite ridiculous. Pope Leo III had fled to Paderborn to the camp of Charlemagne to plead for help and to tell of the wrongs which had been done to him.

37. The Monk is not quoting the original wording of the oath of Pope Leo III, made in Saint Peter's on 23 December 800, but he seems to be aware of it. It is given in full in Philipp Jaffé, *Monumenta Carolina*, Vol. IV, pp. 378–9.

38. Saint Pancras was executed in 295 at the age of fourteen during the Diocletian persecutions. His tomb was a favourite place for making oaths.

39. These words come from the *Liber Pontificalis*, ed. L. Duchesne, 1886, Vol. II, p. 8.

40. cf. Einhard, *The Life of Charlemagne*, §28, p. 81.

41. cf. this curious statement with Bk. II, §9, p. 147.

42. Again cf. Einhard, *The Life of Charlemagne*, §28, p. 81. The Monk is here so much better informed.

43. cf. Einhard, *The Life of Charlemagne*, §26, p. 79.

44. The words 'through the mass of flames' = '... *et per medios flammaram globos* ...'
cf. *Vidimus undantem ruptis fornacibus Aetnam*
     Flammarumque globos *liquefactaque volvere saxa!*
                                             Georgics, I, 472–3.

45. Psalms, 62, 10.

46. cf. Einhard, *The Life of Charlemagne*, §17, p. 71, and §32, p. 85.

47. Liutfrid: no such person seems to have existed.

48. cf. *Aeneid*, III, 618 *et seq.*

49. Exodus, 4, 10.

50. Joshua, 10, 12.
51. Numbers, 27, 22.
52. Matthew, 11, 11.
53. Matthew, 16, 19.
54. Luke, 24, 1–10.
55. Matthew, 25, 29.
56. With this passage, cf. Einhard, *The Life of Charlemagne*, §23, pp. 77–8.
57. The words white linen shirt = *camisia clizana*. cf. Du Cange, II, 399, and III, 532, *sub titulis: cizania, camisia*. The words *glizzum, glezina, glizina* < German *gleysen, gleissen* = to shine white.
58. cf. p. 25. The visit was made in 883, that is just before the Monk wrote this passage.
59. cf. p. 23.
60. cf. p. 23.
61. By the Huns, as always, the Monk means the Avars.
62. Saint Desiderius, or Didier of Autun, was Bishop of Vienne from 596 until his death *c.* 611.
63. This passage, in which Adalbert describes the Nine Rings of the Avars, was translated by Thomas Hodgkin in *Charles the Great*, pp. 155–6. Louis Halphen, *Etudes critiques sur l'histoire de Charlemagne*, Ch. IV, '*Le moine de Saint-Gall*', pp. 134–5, has poured ridicule on what he calls '*la sotte légende de ces neuf lignes de retranchements*', the remains of which no one has ever been able to trace. For him they are derived in the Monk's mind from the nine circles of the Styx in *Aeneid*, VI, 438–9:

> *Fas obstat, tristique palus inamabilis unda*
> *Alligat, et novies Styx interfusa coercet.*

In a letter sent by Charlemagne himself to his Queen Fastrada in 791 and in which the treasures captured from the Avars are described, there is no mention of nine rings. cf. Philipp Jaffé, *Monumenta Carolina*, Vol. IV, *Epistolae Carolinae*, No. 6, p. 349.
64. cf. Einhard, *The Life of Charlemagne*, §13, p. 67.
65. This passage is copied from the *Lorsch Annals*, *sub anno* 795.
66. cf. Einhard, *The Life of Charlemagne*, §8, p. 63.
67. The words '. . . born in a brothel in Burgundy . . .' = *de genicio*

Columbrensi procreati. cf. C. Dezobry and T. Bachelet, *Dictionnaire Général de Biographie et d'Histoire*, 1873, pp. 636, 691, where *ager Columbarensis* = *Le Coulmier* in Burgundy. For *genicium*, *genitium* = *gynaecum*, cf. Du Cange, III, pp. 601–603.

68. cf. Einhard, *The Life of Charlemagne*, §16, p. 70.

69. This means Heito, Bishop of Basel, who went on only one embassy to Constantinople. cf. Einhard, *The Life of Charlemagne*, §33, p. 90.

70. Count Hugo: a name which the Monk has taken from the *Annales regni Francorum, sub anno* 811.

71. The stories in Bk. II, §§5–6, seem to have been inspired by the embassy of Heito, Bishop of Basel, to the court of Nicephorus I, in 811, but by the time Heito arrived in Constantinople Nicephorus was dead and his brother-in-law Michael Rhangabé had replaced him as Emperor. It is known that Heito wrote an account of his embassy, which has since been lost; but the Monk may have been able to consult it.

72. The words '... like the host of heaven ...' = '*instar militiae coelestis*', Acts, 7, 42, or Deuteronomy, 17, 3.

73. Bishop Heito set off on his embassy to Constantinople in 811. If we are now in 812, of Charlemagne's legitimate sons only one, Lewis the Pious, is still alive, and he was twenty-four. What is more, since 800 Charlemagne has had no legal wife.

74. Joshua, 10, 6–7.

75. II Kings, 6, 14.

76. Psalms, 148, 11–12.

77. These are the antiphons called *Antiphonae in Octavas Theophaniae ad Matutinas*, which begin: '*Veterem hominem renovans Salvator venit ad baptismum ...*' with, later on: '*Caput draconis Salvator contrivit in Jordane flumine ...*' Of them J. Lemarié, *La manifestation du Seigneur*, Paris, 1957, p. 520, writes: '*Chantées en grec par des Byzantins en présence de Charlemagne à Aix-la-Chapelle le 13 janvier 802, elles furent sur le champ traduites en latin. On leur conserva leur mélodie originale. Elles furent supprimées lors de la réforme de Pie V.*' The monks of Mount Saint Bernard's Abbey, in a letter dated 18 November 1967, supply the following additional information: 'Though they came into the Latin Church from the Byzantine rite they are today only found in the Armenian rite, and, in the

West, in the Cistercian and Dominican breviaries. They were in the Roman Breviary prior to the 16th-century reform of Pius V. . . . All these antiphons we sing to a rather unusual melody of the 7th mode, and our cantor had previously pointed out . . . that in some places the chant fits rather awkwardly, ignoring the Latin accent.' I am grateful to Fr Lawrence Bagguley, O.A., for help with this note.

78. This remarkable organ was apparently sent in 757 to King Pepin the Short by the Emperor Constantine V. *Vide*, against that year, the entry in the revised *Annales regni Francorum*: '*Misit Constantinus imperator regi Pippino cum aliis donis organum, qui in Franciam usque venit*'; and in the *Lorsch Annals*: '*Venit organus in Francia.*' The Monk has moved the story to 812, in which year envoys from the Emperor Michael I visited Charlemagne. For further details, see W. L. Sumner, *The Organ: Its Evolution, Principles of Construction, and Use*, Macdonald, 3rd edition, 1964, pp. 32–3, and J. Perrot, *L'Orgue, de ses origines hellénistiques à la fin du XIIIe siècle*, Paris, 1965, p. 274 *et seq.* I am grateful to Dr W. L. Sumner for help with this note.

79. The names of these provinces seem to be taken from the *Annales regni Francorum*, *sub annis* 801–802.

80. *Aeneid*, IV, 6.

81. *Aeneid*, IV, 585.

82. Again the Monk commits an extraordinary anachronism. The Persian embassy arrived at Charlemagne's court in 807. Hildigard had been dead since 783!

83. This is the Isembard who appears as a renegade in the fragmentary *chanson-de-geste*, *Gormont et Isembart*, second half of the twelfth century as we have it, ed. A. Payot, *Classiques français du moyen âge*, Paris, 1914. In the poem his father is called Bernard, l. 560.

84. cf. the *Vitâ Sancti Otmari*, cap. 4 *et seq.* in *Monumenta Germaniae Scriptores*, II, 43 *et seq.*

85. This elephant, called Abu-l-Abbas, was sent to Charlemagne by Harun-al-Rachid in 802. It died at Lippenham in Westphalia in 810. In this passage the Monk has added it to the gifts of 807. As with the unguents, so with the animals: he has doubled their species by adding 'some monkeys'. cf. Einhard, *The Life of Charlemagne*, §16, p. 70.

86. These details are taken from the revised *Annales regni Francorum*, year 807. Louis Halphen, op. cit. in n. 65, p. 120, has pointed out how systematically the Monk has added to them. *Annales*: '*Odores atque unguenta et balsamum*'; the Monk: '*Opobalsamum, nardum, unguentaque varia, pigmenta, odoramenta vel medicamenta diversissima*'. He has put them in reverse order, doubled them and added a typical superlative at the end.

87. The words '. . . with strong beer . . .' = *graecingario* = *grucingario* = *grûzzing* (Old High German) = barley beer.

88. cf. the *Annales regni Francorum*, for 801.

89. The words '. . . purple dyestuffs from Spain . . .' = *cum ferrugine Hibera.* cf. '*Pictus acu chlamydem, et ferrugine clarus Ibera.*' *Aeneid*, IX, 582.

90. cf. §26, p. 124.

91. cf. Einhard, *The Life of Charlemagne*, §16, p. 70.

92. Genesis, 15, 18.

93. Virgil, *Bucolics*, I, 63. The River Arar = the Sâone.

94. The words '. . . for every acre of land . . .' = *singulis huobus*.

95. Charlemagne seems not to have understood what his son Lewis the Pious said to him.

96. *The Life of Saint Ambrose* = *Vita Sancti Ambrosii* by Paulinus of Milan, Ch. III: '*Quo facto territus pater ait: "Si vixerit infantulus, aliquid magni erit."*' The Monk writes: '*Si vixerit puerulus iste, aliquid magni erit.*' Charlemagne was presumably speaking Frankish.

97. Hartmut became Abbot in 872 and resigned in 883.

98. This letter was written on 9 April 873.

99. The massacre of the Stellinga, a Saxon tribe, in 842.

100. Charles the Fat had no legitimate heir.

101. cf. Sulpicius Severus, *Vita Sancti Martini*, Ch. 26, ed. C. F. von Halm, *Corpus Scriptorum Ecclesiasticorum Latinorum*, p. 136: '. . . *quamquam etiam inter legendum aut si quid aliud forte agebat numquam animum ab oratione laxabat . . . Ita Martinus etiam, dum aliud agere videretur, semper orabat.*'

102. That is, in Aachen.

103. The oldest parts of St Emmerams-Kirche in Ratisbon, formerly a Benedictine monastery, date back to the eighth century.

104. Proverbs, 20, 8.

105. cf. Einhard, *The Life of Charlemagne*, §14, p. 68, and §17, pp. 71–2
106. ibid. §13, p. 67.
107. As Gaston Paris pointed out, in *Histoire poétique de Charlemagne*, 1865, p. 443, this is an old story, with at least three possible sources.
108. cf. Einhard, *The Life of Charlemagne*, §20, p. 75. Einhard describes the revolt of Pepin the Hunchback before the conspiracy of Hardrad, but he is careful to point out that in effect the second came first; the Monk follows the order of Einhard, but omits to observe the word *prius*.
109. Genesis, 6, 4.
110. The fact that Ratisbon was the scene of the conspiracy by Pepin the Hunchback and that the cleric who revealed it was called Fardulf is given in the revised *Annales regni Francorum, sub anno* 792.
111. This story was first told of Thrasybulus, tyrant of Miletus, in Asia Minor. Livy tells it about King Tarquin, I, 54. It was no doubt from Livy that the Monk took it. There are other possible sources, e.g. the *Facta ac Dicta Memorabilia* of Valerius Maximus, VII, 4.
112. Prüm, near Trier, on the Moselle, a Benedictine house founded 720 and destroyed by the Norsemen in 882, just before the Monk started writing.
113. Charles the Fat had no legitimate heir. Very shortly after the Monk wrote this sentence, the Emperor tried to persuade the Pope to legitimize this bastard son Bernard, but without success. cf. *Annales Fuldenses, sub anno* 885.
114. Eishere, from *eis + here*, terrifying + army.
115. Deuteronomy, 2, 10.
116. Judges, 2, 22.
117. This cattle pest is recorded in the revised *Annales regni Francorum, sub anno* 810.
118. cf. Einhard, *The Life of Charlemagne*, §14, p. 68.
119. See the Book of Judith, in the Apocrypha.
120. Judges, 7, 2.
121. This extraordinary story is made the more odd by the fact that the Monk seems to be confusing Charlemagne with his grandfather Charles Martel.

122. Carloman, King of Bavaria and Italy, and the older brother of Charles the Fat, died 22 September 880.

123. Arnulf, Duke of Carinthia, the illegitimate son of Carloman, born *c.* 850, succeeded to his uncle Charles the Fat as King of Germany in 887, became Emperor in 896 and died 899. He was buried in St Emmerams-Kirche in Ratisbon, which is mentioned on p. 152.

124. cf. n. 229. Tiny twig, indeed, and one who was to cause much trouble to Arnulf, the 'small bough', his first cousin and like himself illegitimate.

125. This passage, which is very thin, is taken from the revised *Annales regni Francorum*, for the years 753, 755.

126. Pepin the Short never visited Rome. The Monk has adapted these words from the *Annales regni Francorum, sub anno* 774: '*orandi gratia Romam proficiscitur*'. Unfortunately the annalist was writing about Charlemagne, not Pepin the Short.

127. Thomas Hodgkin discusses this anecdote in *Italy and her Invaders, 744-774*, Vol. VII, pp. 300-301, and translates part of it.

128. This is not so. Pepin of Herstal is given a brief mention by Bede in the *Ecclesiastical History*, V, 10-11.

129. The first campaign against the Longobards was in 773. Charlemagne married the daughter of King Desiderius in 770. As so often, the Monk has his facts back to front.

130. This Otker really fled from the court of Carloman with that King's widow Gerberga, and he was in Verona and not Pavia at this moment. *Otkerus* is the Monk's adaptation of *Autcarius* in the *Liber Pontificalis*, ed. L. Duchesne, 1886, Vol. I, pp. 488 and 495, which he seems to be following here.

131. It is thought that the Monk is here following the letter of a certain Catulf, dated *c.* 775, in which the last stages of the siege of Pavia are mentioned, cf. Philipp Jaffé, *Monumenta Carolina*, Vol. IV, pp. 336-41, especially p. 337.

132. cf. Sulpicius Severus, *Dialogi*, II, i, edited by C. F. von Halm, *Corpus Scriptorum Ecclesiasticorum Latinorum*, p. 181: '... *bigerricam vestem, brevem atque hispidam, quinque comparatam argenteis ... Cum hac igitur oblaturus sacrificium Deo veste procedit.*'

133. Isaiah, 51, 1.

134. The details concerning Lewis the Pious are adapted from the

De gestis Domini Lodewici Imperatoris by Thegan, Bishop of Trier.

135. I Kings, 2, 12.
136. The words 'old shirts' = *camisilia*.
137. The words 'to make tunics' = *in modum sepium*.
138. The words 'to be run up as overalls' = *in modum vitium pastinari*.
139. This long passage has been printed in English by Douglas Woodruff, *Charlemagne*, pp. 60–62, but he is using the translation of A. J. Grant.
140. Galatians, 3, 27.
141. Romans, 6, 3.
142. Hebrews, 6, 6.
143. Acts, 4, 34.

BIBLIOGRAPHY

I. MODERN EDITIONS

1829: Pertz, G. H., *Monumenta Germaniae Historica, Scriptores*, Vol. II, pp. 443–65, Berlin.

1840: Teulet, A., *Oeuvres complètes d'Eginhard*, Vol. I, pp. 2–115, with translation, Paris (*Société de l'Histoire de France*).

1867: Jaffé, Philipp, *Einharti Vita Caroli Magni*, pp. 487–541 of *Bibliotheca Rerum Germanicarum*, Vol. IV, *Monumenta Carolina*, Berlin.

1867: Jaffé, Philipp, *Monachus Sangallensis de Carolo Magno*, pp. 628–700 of *Bibliotheca Rerum Germanicarum*, Vol. IV, *Monumenta Carolina*, Berlin.

1880: Waitz, G., *Einharti Vita Karoli Magni*, Hanover (*Scriptores Rerum Germanicarum in usum scholarum*).

1911: Holder-Egger, O., *Einhardi Vita Karoli Magni*, Hanover (*Scriptores Rerum Germanicarum in usum scholarum*).

1915: Garrod, H. W., and Mowat, R. B., *Einhard's Life of Charlemagne* (Oxford).

1918: Meyer von Knonau, G., *Monachus Sangallensis (Notkerus Balbulus) de Carolo Magno*, Vol. VI in *St Gallische Geschichtsquellen*, St Gallen.

1938: Halphen, Louis, *Eginhard, Vie de Charlemagne*, Paris (*Classiques de l'Histoire de France au Moyen Age*).

II. TRANSLATIONS

1840: Teulet, A., *Oeuvres complètes d'Eginhard*, Vol. I, pp. 2–115, with text, Paris (*Société de l'Histoire de France*).

1920: Abel, O., revised by M. Tangl, *Kaiser Karls Leben von Einhard*, 4th edition, Leipzig (*Geschichtschreiber der deutschen Vorzeit*).

1922: Grant, A. J., *Early Lives of Charlemagne by Eginhard and the Monk of St. Gall* (The King's Classics).

1938: Halphen, Louis, *Eginhard, Vie de Charlemagne*, Paris (*Classiques de l'Histoire de France au Moyen Age*).

1960: Painter, Sidney, *The Life of Charlemagne by Einhard* (University of Michigan).

III. CRITICAL WORKS

1897: Hodgkin, Thomas, *Charles the Great*, London.

1898: Monod, Gabriel, *Etudes critiques sur les Sources de l'Histoire Carolingienne*, Paris.

1899: Davis, H. W. C., *Charlemagne, the Hero of Two Nations* (Heroes of the Nations series).

1899: Hodgkin, Thomas, *Italy and her Invaders*, Vol. VII, Book VIII, *Frankish Invasions* (Oxford).

1899: Hodgkin, Thomas, *Italy and her Invaders*, Vol. VIII, Book IX, *The Frankish Empire* (Oxford).

1921: Halphen, Louis, *Etudes critiques sur l'Histoire de Charlemagne*, Paris.

1924: Ganshof, F. L., 'Notes critiques sur Eginhard, biographe de Charlemagne', article in *Revue Belge de Philologie et d'Histoire*, Vol. III pp. 725–58.

1934: Kleinclausz, A., *Charlemagne*, Paris.

1942: Kleinclausz, A., *Eginhard*, Paris.

1945: Calmette, Joseph, *Charlemagne, sa vie et son oeuvre*, Paris.

1947: Halphen, Louis, *Charlemagne et l'Empire Carolingien*, Paris.

1949: Ganshof, F. L., *The Imperial Coronation of Charlemagne* (Sixteenth David Murray Foundation Lecture), Glasgow.

1950: Folz, Robert, *Le Souvenir et la Légende de Charlemagne, dans l'Empire Germanique Médiéval*, Paris.

1956: Winston, Richard, *Charlemagne* (Eyre & Spottiswoode).

1958: Ganshof, F. L., *La Belgique Carolingienne*, Brussels.

1965: Bullough, Donald, *The Age of Charlemagne* (Elek Books).

INDEX

The index which follows includes every proper name and place-name which is mentioned in the two lives of Charlemagne written by Einhard and by Notker the Stammerer, Monk of Saint Gall. Under these headwords I have also listed in note form the events which concern each person and place.

*

MORE ABOUT PENGUINS
AND PELICANS

Penguinews, which appears every month, contains details of all the new books issued by Penguins as they are published. From time to time it is supplemented by *Penguins in Print*, which includes almost 5,000 titles.

A specimen copy of *Penguinews* will be sent to you free on request. Please write to Dept EP, Penguin Books Ltd, Harmondsworth, Middlesex, for your copy.

In the U.S.A.: For a complete list of books available from Penguins in the United States write to Dept CS, Penguin Books, 625 Madison Avenue, New York, New York 10022.

In Canada: For a complete list of books available from Penguins in Canada write to Penguin Books Canada Ltd, 2801 John Street, Markham, Ontario L3R 1B4.

Translated by Lewis Thorpe

GREGORY OF TOURS

THE HISTORY OF THE FRANKS

Gregory of Tours (*c.* A.D. 539–594) intended his *History* to be a chronicle of the events which led up to and included the twenty-one years he spent as Bishop of Tours. This volume contains all ten books of the *History*, the last seven describing Gregory's own time (in which he played an important role) and particularly the quarrels of four of the sons of Lothar I and the machinations of the ruthless Queen Fredegund, third wife of Chilperic. As he unravels the bewildering events of these decades, what emerges is no dry historical document, but a vivid and dramatic narrative of French history in the sixth century.

GEOFFREY OF MONMOUTH

THE HISTORY OF THE KINGS OF BRITAIN

It is difficult to say whether Geoffrey of Monmouth, in writing his famous *Historia Regum Britanniae*, relied more on the old chroniclers or on a gift for romantic invention. However, leaving aside its merits as history, his heroic epic of such half-legendary kings as Cymbeline, Arthur and Lear enjoyed great popularity and served to inspire Malory, Spenser and Shakespeare, among other writers.